"I WAS LETTERING LABELS FOR HANNAH'S CUBBY WHEN THE YELLING BEGAN. THERE WERE PIERCING SCREAMS FOLLOWED BY SILENCE. THEN THE SCREAMS AGAIN, MIXED WITH DEEP, THROAT-CATCHING SOBS."

Hannah, her body draped in a woman's house-dress, with filth on her face and gum in her hair, seemed more like a savage animal than an eight-year-old girl, using gutteral noises rather than words, and viciously lashing out at any human touch.

Mary MacCracken was at first resentful at having Hannah thrust into her class, and more than a little afraid of the threat Hannah posed to her competence.

Both teacher and child had a long way to go. And there was just one way they could make it:

Together. . . .

LOVEY

"A triumph!"—*Publishers Weekly*

"You will remember it long after the last page . . . an inspiring book as well as a delight to read."—*Pittsburgh Press*

"A story that will tug at the heart of anyone who has ever loved a child."
—*Literary Guild Magazine*

SIGNET Books You'll Want to Read

Lovey

A Very Special Child

by
Mary MacCracken

A SIGNET BOOK
NEW AMERICAN LIBRARY
TIMES MIRROR

NAL BOOKS ARE ALSO AVAILABLE AT DISCOUNTS IN BULK
QUANTITY FOR INDUSTRIAL OR SALES-PROMOTIONAL USE.
FOR DETAILS, WRITE TO PREMIUM MARKETING DIVISION,
NEW AMERICAN LIBRARY, INC., 1301 AVENUE OF THE
AMERICAS, NEW YORK, NEW YORK 10019.

Library of Congress Catalog Card Number: 76-15389

This is an authorized reprint of a hardcover edition published
by J. B. Lippincott Company.

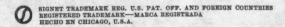
SIGNET, SIGNET CLASSICS, MENTOR, PLUME AND MERIDIAN BOOKS
are published by The New American Library, Inc.,
1301 Avenue of the Americas, New York, New York 10019

FIRST SIGNET PRINTING, OCTOBER, 1977

1 2 3 4 5 6 7 8 9

PRINTED IN THE UNITED STATES OF AMERICA

For my remarkable father,
Clifford Wilcox Burnham,
and Anne

LOVEY:

A Very Special Child

"Wait just a minute, Mary. I want to talk to you." The Director covered the phone and nodded toward the coffeepot. "Pour yourself a cup. I'll be right with you."

I hesitated, juggling the armload of books and old magazines I'd brought in. I didn't want to stop now. This was the first day of school and the children would be arriving in a few minutes. I wanted to get down to my room, put away these last things, and make sure everything was ready.

"Well, now, everything set?" the Director said as she hung up.

"I think so, except for these books and maybe a few travel posters that I'll tack up until the kids get some paintings done." Our children were even more sensitive than most to the climate of their surroundings. I wanted no rush, no hurry, no hel-ter-skelter when they first arrived. The Director understood this as well as I did. Why was she keeping me here, diddling around and chatting?

"Uh, Mary, I wanted to tell you . . . there's been a change in your class."

"A change? What do you mean? What's wrong? Has something happened to one of the children?"

"No, no. Nothing like that. It's just that I've re-arranged things a little."

I was instantly on guard. Euphemisms from the Director were always a danger sign. "Rearranged things?"

"Yes. Last night when I went over the class lists I decided to put Hannah Rosnic in with you and move Carolyn—"

"Hannah Rosnic!" I interrupted. "How can that work? Brian and Rufus are almost ready for regular school—Brian's twelve; this is his last year—and even Jamie is able to sit long enough to do some reading. Carolyn will fit in beautifully, I know she will. We took her on trips with us last year. I know she's withdrawn, and her fantasies—"

"I've put Carolyn in Ellen's class," the Director interrupted in her turn. "I realized last night that it was asking too much of Ellen to take on Hannah. Ellen's too new. She's right for her other three and she'll be good with Carolyn. But Hannah will be better off with you."

"Listen," I said. "What about the boys? And I don't even know Hannah—except what I heard from down the hall last year. I don't have any rapport with her. How am I going to get anything going between her and the boys? What makes you think they'll accept her at all?"

The Director sipped her coffee and lit a cigarette, fanning the smoke away from her eyes. She looked exactly as she always had, cheerful, dynamic, the strong sinewy cords in her neck softened by her feathery white hair. "I've thought about it. The boys will be good for her, give her a nice balance." She paused and smiled at me. "And Hannah'll stir them up a little—give your room a little more excitement."

"Excitement? What do we need with excitement? We've all come a long way, but it's possible that we could lose everything we've gained so far with Hannah in there."

"Anything's possible," the Director said coolly. The phone rang. She picked up my untouched coffee and her half-empty cup and headed back to her desk, nodding to me and dismissing me at the same time. "Well, that's set, then. Fine. I'll send Hannah down when she arrives."

I gathered up my books and magazines and went out into the hall. What was I going to do? All I knew about Hannah Rosnic was that she had come to our school sometime in the middle of last year and had been in Shirley's class at the end of the hall. I'd seen her, fat, dumpy, and dirty, on the playground, and I'd heard her, screaming and howling from her classroom. But that was all, except for a few dim memories of discussions at staff meetings. And now she was going to be one of my four!

A last-minute change like this was unprecedented. Ours was a school for children with severe emotional disturbances. Each of our children was unique, with such individual problems as well as strengths that what was planned to help one child deal with anger and hurt and isolation would be useless to another. What I had prepared for Carolyn would never work for Hannah.

And yet, this was what was going to happen. Once the Director had made up her mind, she wouldn't argue and there was no point in trying to discuss it. If she had decided to move Hannah into my classroom, Hannah would be there.

I opened the door to my room and immediately my spirits rose. It was a beautiful room, facing south, large, sunny, and bright. One of the school's trustees had arranged for us to use this church building, rent free, while we waited for our new school to be built. This particular Sunday-school room had previously been off limits to us. It was the church's pride and joy, full of play equipment, rugs, tables, even an easel for painting. One whole wall was open to sunlight, with five floor-to-ceiling windows. Best of all, there was a door opening onto the driveway outside. There is absolutely nothing better than a door of your own to the outside world. Compared to the cold, barren rooms I'd taught in before, this was heaven.

Brian was the first to arrive. He came so quietly that if I hadn't been watching I wouldn't have known he was there. He came to the hall door and stood just outside it, his hands hidden in his pockets so I couldn't tell whether they were trembling or not. Each year I think I've outgrown the ridiculous soaring excitement that I felt the first time I came to the school and saw the children.

And then each year I find I'm wrong. The same spine-jolting, rocking delight hits me and spins me around, and I have to be careful not to somersault across the room when the children come.

"Hey, Brian, I'm glad to see you." I walked across the room toward him, waiting for his smile, thin and sweet, to come and warm his pointed little face.

But Brian didn't smile. He didn't even come into the room. "Why are we in here?" he asked. "This isn't our room. This isn't where we were last year."

It's so hard for our children to handle new situations. Their sense of self is so small, their beings so fragile, that if their outer surroundings change, they fear that they themselves will fall apart.

"Listen," I said. "This is the best room we've ever had. Don't spurn luxury. Look, we've got a whole coat closet, instead of just hooks."

Brian took a step or two into the room and peered at the coat closet. "I liked just the hooks," he said.

"And we've got blocks and trucks and a whole toy kitchen—a stove and a sink and tables—and now, look here, our own door. How about that? No more having to go through the office when we want to sneak out before lunch to ride our bikes."

Brian was all the way in the room now. "Do we still have the bikes?"

"Sure. We've even got a couple of new ones." They weren't really new, the church ladies and the Junior Leaguers had donated them, but they were new to us.

Within the next minute Rufus arrived. He looked tan and healthy and had obviously had a good summer.

"Hey, Mary," he announced, "maybe we're going to get a cat. I'm almost not 'lergic any more and my mom says as soon as I'm not 'lergic we can get one." He turned toward Brian. "And I'll bring it in here, Brian, so you can see it."

Rufus walked comfortably around the room, commenting on everything, and I could see Brian loosening up, his fears diminishing. The children did so much for each other without realizing it. Rufus's explorations freed Brian to begin his own, and soon both boys were settled on the floor taking out the books and papers and small supplies that I'd put in their individual cubbies.

Jamie, the last of my three boys, burst through the classroom door and half rocked, half ran, across the room.

I sat down fast. Jamie was eight and I'd only had him for one year. He was still potentially explosive, and the more body contact he got during times of stress, the better. A new room plus the first day of school added up to a lot of pressure.

A huge grin stretched over Jamie's face as he spotted me and headed straight on. I spread my legs as wide as I could to make a big lap and opened my arms. Without caution, without a pause in his breakneck run, Jamie took a flying leap and landed squarely in my lap.

"Hey ho, Jamie," I said, wrapping him up in my arms. "What took you so long?"

Jamie didn't say anything, but then he rarely did. He just buried his head against my neck while I rocked him back and forth. Pretty soon he came up for air and surveyed the room from his safe station. Then, seeing Brian and Rufus contentedly sorting the contents of their cubbies and realizing that he could stay where he was as long as he wanted, he gradually began to disentangle himself: first an arm, then another arm, then a foot, then the other—one quick turn around my chair, back on my lap, off again, this time to a chair of his own.

By ten o'clock the room began to be ours. The boys had taken everything out of their cubbies and put it back again at least a dozen times—touching, feeling, even smelling everything before they were convinced that it really belonged to them. Jamie had tried out every chair in the classroom before he finally settled on one and thereafter carried it with him wherever he went.

I'd cleaned out Carolyn's cubby as unobtrusively as possible and was lettering new labels for Hannah's cubby and hook in the coat closet when the yelling began. At first it was muffled; then the noise became louder, closer. There were piercing screams followed by silence. Then the screams began again, mixed with deep, throat-catching sobs.

Was that Hannah? Had she arrived? If so, where was she? The Director had said she'd send her down when she came. It was ten thirty. Surely she must have arrived by now.

A moment later the Director stood in our doorway. "Good morning, boys." She smiled. "Isn't this a lovely room? I see you're working hard already. Mary, may I speak to you for a minute?"

I walked over to where the Director stood by the hall door. She lowered her voice as she spoke.

"Hannah's down in her old classroom. I don't seem to be able to get her to leave and join you, and I wondered if you'd step down there for a minute or two."

I didn't want to go. Things were just getting started in our room; tension and anxiety were gradually seeping out. Fears could return too easily if the boys were suddenly left alone. Still, the screaming and sobbing were clearer now that the door was open—and that couldn't go on.

"Will you cover for me till I get back?" I asked the Director. She nodded and I went over and squatted down next to Brian. "Bri, I have to go down the hall. The Director's going to stay here while I'm gone. I won't be long, okay?"

I studied his face. He didn't smile, but there was no sign of panic. He just nodded and turned back to his book. The Director sat down beside Jamie near the record player. Everything seemed to be all right.

I closed the door and mentally crossed my fingers; so much depended on the first day. If the children began to feel safe and relaxed in the room and with each other, a great deal of time could be saved.

The hall was no longer quiet. It was filled with the good sounds of school: chairs being pushed across the floor, record players set at various volumes, doors opening, closing, teachers speaking softly, a few children's voices, a little laughter. Only Hannah's screams sliced through the air, dividing time into short, painful segments.

I stopped outside the back classroom and looked through the window. The new teacher, Ellen, had bolted the door, and for a minute I wished I hadn't come. This was the room I'd first taught in when I was hired as a substitute five years before. I stood outside, remembering how inexperienced I'd been. My first act had been to unbolt the door, my second to fall flat on my face as I held onto a runaway child. But we'd both learned, and the door had stayed unlocked. Locks and cages were never meant for children, and I felt both sorrow and frustration to see the door bolted again.

As I looked through the window I could see that Hannah had barricaded herself inside the wooden jungle gym that was wedged into a far corner. She clung to the bars, alternately screaming and sobbing, her face contorted with pain or rage or perhaps fear. The other children stood gaping at her, but if they ventured near she reached through the wooden rungs and swiped at them with her hand.

I tapped on the window. Ellen looked up and her round, sweet face flooded with relief as she hurried to the door, unlocked it, and drew me inside.

"Am I ever glad to see you," she said. "This has been going on for over an hour. Nothing helps. Somehow Hannah got away from the Director this morning and ran in here. I guess she was expecting to see her teacher from last year, because when she saw me she went crazy, yelling and tearing at my clothes as if she thought she'd find her old teacher somewhere underneath. Finally she gave up and climbed into the jungle gym, and now she won't let anybody near her." Ellen lowered her voice. "Listen, Mary, you've got to get her out of here. She's scaring the other kids half to death. I've tried everything I can think of and she just gets worse."

I looked over toward Hannah. She seemed smaller than I'd remembered, but what Ellen said was true—she was getting worse. Her sobs and screams were louder, deeper than ever. How could she keep it up for so long? In spite of everything, I felt a surge of admiration. Somewhere inside this child there must be tremendous strength.

I walked toward the jungle gym, not sure what to do, only trying to get a feel, a sense, of Hannah. I hadn't been anxious to have her in my classroom—Carolyn would have made things much easier. Still, if she was going to be with us, I had to get to know her. What must it be like to come back and find your teacher gone when you thought she'd be there? What was it like to be eight years old and hurt and angry and confused? If I were Hannah, what would I want, what would I need?

As I approached, Hannah began stamping her feet. It was as if her vocal cords were already making all the noise they could and now, with a new danger, she needed another source of sound.

Two sides of the jungle gym were against the walls. Hannah clung to the third side, shaking it and stamping her feet. With no plan at all, I climbed up the fourth side.

Hannah's screaming stopped and I took advantage of her surprise to reach the top, away from her clawing fingers. I lay flat on the top platform, trying to listen with my whole being, not just my ears. Nothing. There was absolutely no sound from below. I leaned over the platform and there was Hannah, bent over, her head pressed against the bars, great pink wads of gum stuck in the red-gold of her hair. I talked to the back of her small, grimy neck.

"Hiya, Hannah."

There wasn't any answer, not a twitch of response, but somehow I had the feeling that she'd heard me.

"Listen," I continued. "This isn't your class. You're supposed to be with us, in the room down the hall on the other side. We've been waiting for you down there."

Hannah didn't make a sound, but she turned her head just a fraction of an inch. I went on.

"Shirley, your teacher last year, didn't want to leave. She liked our school and she liked teaching you. But her husband was studying to be a doctor and he was sent to a hospital a long way away— and so she had to stop teaching here to go with him."

The muscles in my neck were getting tired from dangling my head over the edge of the platform, and I longed to get down and stand beside her, get a closer look, maybe even hold onto her square, solid body and let some of her anger drain out. But Hannah seemed nowhere near ready. I was going to have to wait.

Suddenly she turned and twisted her neck and body to peer up at me. For an instant she hung outside the wooden bars with her face turned up toward me and then she was gone, out of the jungle gym, out of the door that Ellen had left unlocked when she let me in, and down the hall. I climbed down quickly and followed. Ellen's door clicked behind me and the bolt slid back in place.

Hannah ran up and down, back and forth in the hall, like a fat mouse in a maze. She was dressed in a woman's cotton housedress that was tied at the waist with a string. The dress reached to the tops of her heavy brown shoes and she stumbled around, banging against the walls, letting out periodic snarling howls. Once she turned back toward me and I could see that both her face and the front of her dress were wet—stained with tears, or sweat, or maybe both. She opened the door to our room, more by accident than design. The boys and the Director stood up simultaneously as Hannah crashed in. I was only a step behind and closed the door behind me. We needed a little space, a little time to ourselves.

It was hard to tell who was more frightened, Hannah or the boys. They stared at each other silently until the Director called out cheerily, "Well, Hannah, I see you've found your room. Good enough. Now that we're all set, I'll get back to work. Phone never stops ringing, a thousand things to do. Have a good day."

The Director was out the hall door and gone before any of us moved, but just as the door clicked shut Hannah ran toward it. Brian and Rufus had huddled together in front of the outside door. Jamie whimpered and ran to where I stood by the hall door and buried his head against my legs. Without previous planning, we had formed a barricade to the exits. There was no out for Hannah. Like it or not, she was with us.

Hannah backtracked and then made one dash for the hall door, and I captured her as she came by. "Gotcha. Enough now, okay?"

I said it as much to reassure the boys as to steady Hannah, but while it may have helped them to hear a familiar tone in the room it did nothing for her. She slid out of my arms to the floor, propped herself on her hands and knees inside her long housedress, and with a moaning, keening noise began rocking back and forth, back and forth, like a tormented infant in a crib.

The safety we had begun to build was gone. Trouble, trauma, violence, and fear had invaded our room. I muttered a silent expletive in the direction of the departed Director, but it wasn't of any use. She was gone; Hannah was here. We'd just have to get through somehow.

I turned to the boys. "Hannah's going to be in our class this year. She feels badly about missing her old teacher and some other things. It's going to take a while for us to get used to each other, but it's going to be okay. We just need a little time. Now let's get busy. Rufus, Brian, bring your books on over here and let's see what we're going to be working on."

As I spoke there was a dull, heavy thud and I turned back toward Hannah. She was not only rocking, she was banging her head, bringing it down hard against the black tile floor at the end of each forward thrust. I knew that part of this head banging was to test us, but part of it was also an attempt to destroy the torments inside her.

I sat down on the floor next to Hannah and pushed my leg beneath her head to cushion the blow. "No. In this room you don't hurt yourself or anyone else. And no one hurts you. You can rock if you have to, but no banging."

She brought her head down again, drove it hard into my thigh—and then, as the noon whistle wailed, suddenly she was still. We sat without speaking. I leaned against the wall with Hannah spread out, drenched in sweat, inert against my leg, while the three boys watched us silently from the other side of our room.

2

Jamie was the last to leave our room that first day. We were both limp from emotion and heat, and we sat in a chair by the windows watching for his bus. But as soon as his driver arrived and he was safely aboard, I went down to the office, unlocked the file cabinet, and took out Hannah's folder.

The Director was in the office, a calm oasis in the midst of confused bus drivers, anxious mothers, and tired teachers. She was at her best here, soothing and at the same time encouraging. She had founded the school fifteen years before and had worked harder and harder each year, raising money to keep the doors open, raising standards, coping with the ever-increasing publicity, the long waiting lists of children. Finally, with the death of her husband, the school had become her life. For years it had existed in rented and borrowed buildings, but now the dream was almost reality: Within a few months ground would be broken for a spacious new school building, built to the Director's specifications. Nothing escaped her, and she nodded to me as I took Hannah's file back to the quiet of my own room.

I spread the folder out on one of the tables before the open windows. Small air currents stirred through the room and riffled the edges of the papers. I was eager to read the reports, hoping to discover what had happened to make Hannah so angry, so frightened. She was more like a young animal than a little girl. Why wouldn't she let anyone near her? Where had the rage and self-destruction come from?

The folder contained a school form filled out by Mrs. Rosnic, a health form from the pediatrician, a report from the principal to the public school Hannah had attended; there were also a joint report by a psychologist and a social worker at a mental health clinic, a final report by another psychologist from the public school, and a half-page year-end report written by Hannah's teacher from last year. From these I gradually pieced together Hannah's history.

She had been born eight years earlier in a hospital in New York City. Her life had been filled with violence from the beginning. She had cried constantly through her first days and nights, eating little at first, finally refusing to eat at all. In desperation, Mrs. Rosnic took her back to the hospital where she had been born. They discovered an abdominal obstruction which had caused food blockage and dehydration. Hannah was operated on and hospitalized for several weeks.

When she returned home she was able to eat and some of the screaming stopped, but she rocked back and forth in her crib, banging her head against the end panel.

Her brother, Carl, three years older, was resentful of the new baby. One day soon after Hannah came home from the hospital, Mrs. Rosnic found Carl by Hannah's crib, hitting her on the head again and again. In spite of everything, she grew; she walked at thirteen months and completed toilet training at age two. However, Mrs. Rosnic continued to bottle-feed her until she was three years old, and although no connection was made, it seemed pertinent to me that Hannah didn't try to talk until then. Her speech consisted primarily of grunts and monosyllables that only Mrs. Rosnic could understand.

When Hannah was four, her family moved to the run-down industrial city where she still lived. They occupied a two-family house in a derelict section of town. Mrs. Rosnic's father lived downstairs; the Rosnics themselves occupied the second floor.

Hannah's father had been a strange, brutal man. He must have been tortured by both emotional and physical ailments. The records showed that he had been in and out of mental institutions over the years, yelling, shouting, beating his children when he was home. Later he was confined to a wheelchair, from which he berated the world and everyone in it. He died in the same bizarre

manner in which he had lived. Rising suddenly
up out of his wheelchair at his mother's funeral,
he was stricken with a heart attack and died the
next day, two years before Hannah came to our
school.

At the time of her husband's death, Mrs. Rosnic
was pregnant with a third child. Still in her early
thirties, a widow with little money and no training, with an ailing, demanding father, two young
children, and another child soon to be born, she
became ill herself, overcome by a deep depression.

She turned to her church for help; they put her
in touch with a community mental health center.
Here she was interviewed jointly by a psychiatric
social worker and a psychologist, who judged her
to be of "bright normal intellect with fair insight
and judgment, but with a feeling of being unable
to cope."

I got up from the table and began to pace as I
read. Who wouldn't feel "unable to cope" under
similar conditions? The report ambled on, bleak
and without compassion. Carl, Hannah's brother,
was summarized and dismissed in two brief sentences as having "a childhood adjustment problem with the unusual phobia of fearing the key to
an old clock." Hannah was described as "a seven-
year-old Caucasian female—"

I put the report down, hating the stilted language. Who could write that? And why? Was it
to impress some invisible audience or was it simply

the way psychologists had been taught to write reports? Hannah was a sad, solid, gutsy little girl with blue eyes and red-gold hair. How could they write "seven-year-old Caucasian female"? Why did people deal out labels instead of looking at a child? Never mind. Forget the anger. It didn't help now.

"—Caucasian female exhibiting restless behavior, with unintelligible speech consisting primarily of grunting noises. Judgment and insight extremely poor. Diagnosis: Psychosis. Organic brain disease versus schizophrenia."

It seemed to me a dangerous, presumptuous diagnosis after one brief interview. I searched the remaining pages for more concrete information. An electroencephalogram had been made, and since it was within normal limits Hannah was put in a kindergarten class on a trial basis—but this lasted only a short time. Soon she was put on home instruction because of her "disruptive behavior." The dates in the reports were confusing, but it must have been a hard, bleak period for Mrs. Rosnic, for the whole family.

I shook my head. No wonder the teachers in our school rarely complained. Our troubles, whatever they were, were small compared to the lives of our children and their families.

The late-afternoon sky was dark and the air was filled with the musty smell of rain. At least it would be cooler tomorrow. Tomorrow? Tomorrow would be here very soon and I still had a great deal to do before morning. I turned on the overhead light and skimmed the remaining pages.

Mrs. Rosnic's pregnancy had gone full term and Helen had been born, a healthy eight-pound girl. Hannah had remained on home instruction until a place was found for her here; then one last psychological work-up was done in the public school. It said that Hannah—an aggressive child with a deep underlying pathology—seemed to be living completely in a world of her own. "This child must be regarded as a threat to other children."

Lightning streaked across the sky. No one else was left at school and I knew I should hurry.

How could a child ever grow in a place where she was looked upon as a threat? There was only one positive note in the report: The psychologist noted that Hannah's drawings showed "an above-average mentality."

Well, maybe this was how I'd have to reach her, through her mind, her intelligence. But how could I get through? She'd fought so many enemies already in her eight years, seen more pain and cruelty than most of us do in a lifetime. Her mind must be sealed behind many layers—she would have needed to build thick walls in order to survive as long as she had.

Outside, the rain pelted hard against the black macadam. I closed my windows and read the last remaining page. The report from Hannah's teacher of last year described Hannah as a troubled, sad little girl, unable or unwilling to use eating utensils, given to long crying spells and temper tantrums, her speech a garble of unintelligible slurred consonants—and yet her actions showed an acute awareness of her environment. She had remained difficult and disruptive throughout the year, but there had been some improvement and rapport gradually developed between teacher and child.

It must have been a cruel blow for Hannah to come back this morning and find her teacher gone, the first semblance of security disrupted. Whatever tiny hope had stayed alive inside her must have crashed into despair.

I put the report on the top shelf of my closet and left by my own door. I stood on the stoop just outside and watched the small rivers of rain swirl past; then I took off my shoes and raced up the driveway to the parking lot in my bare feet. But when I reached my car, I stood still for a minute before getting in. My dress and hair were already soaked and the rain felt cool and clean against my face and arms. I wished that it would cool my head and heart as well. Hannah would bring enough passion into our room. She would need a teacher who was clear and steady and strong.

What I needed to do, had to do as soon as possible, was set up an appointment with Mrs. Rosnic so that we could talk. There were so many complicating factors in Hannah's history: the operation, the isolation of the hospital, the head blows, the brutal father, the prolonged bottle feeding. I was as confused as when I started.

3

"Good morning, Rufus," I said as we arrived together the next day. "How's it going?"

But his ebullience of yesterday morning was gone. He sat down glumly and peered at me through his horn-rimmed glasses without answering my question. Instead he asked, "Is that girl going back to her other class?"

"Hannah? Hannah doesn't have another class. She was only in the other room yesterday by mistake. This is her regular room."

Rufus looked down at his feet. "I don't like her. I don't like her in here. She ruins everything."

I sat down beside Rufus. I knew how he felt. I'd said almost the same thing to the Director. "Hannah's had a really tough time . . ." I began.

Rufus got up from the table. "I don't want to talk about her!" he shouted at me. "I hate her! Don't you understand that? I hate her and I don't want to talk about her!"

"Okay," I said. "Okay. What do you want to talk about?"

"Nothing." Rufus kicked the table leg with the toe of his shoe. "I just want it to be the way it was last year, without that dummy girl."

It wasn't just Hannah. It was always hard for the kids when a new child came. With only four children in a class, we were so much a part of each other that what one did profoundly affected the others. The children's usual stay at the school was for three years, although if they were making good progress and had not yet reached their thirteenth birthday they were sometimes allowed to stay for a longer period. This was Rufus's fourth year, and he had been in my class from the start.

When he had come to our school three years before, he had looked more like a middle-aged businessman than an eight-year-old boy. He wore a dark suit and heavy horn-rimmed glasses, and his hair was combed flat against his head. He carried a large brown briefcase and he'd talked to his briefcase most of the first weeks, crouching nervously behind a bookcase.

Rufus was scared of the world, the school, and himself. He was intelligent and he used his intelligence to manipulate the world, which only made it more frightening. Illness was his control. Anything that Rufus thought might prove unpleasant or difficult was met with a stomachache. Usually this meant that he stayed home or got special attention, which was what he'd wanted in the first place.

But gradually Rufus had grown stronger and more independent. Occasionally, under stress, he still talked to an imaginary companion, and sometimes when things went badly at home he wet his bed. But Rufus was growing all the time. If there was a leader in our classroom, it was Rufus.

Now that Rufus had started talking, he kept on. "She's a dummy girl. She can't even talk and she's fat and she's dirty."

Any new child is difficult, but a child like Hannah is a triple threat. She not only claimed my attention and destroyed the safety of our classroom, she also reminded the boys of how fragile they were themselves. If one child in the room could shatter, so could they all.

Rufus gave the chair another kick. "Why does she yell like that? Why don't you make her stop?"

"I'm trying, Ruf. Believe me, I'm trying. Just give her a little time; give us all a little time. First days are hard. Remember Jamie last year? He yelled and kicked and ran away whenever he could. I know Hannah's hard, but it's only the second day and maybe today will be better."

By nine thirty my attempt at optimism was fading. The boys were there but they were tense, and there was no sign of Hannah at all. Rufus was rubbing his stomach as if recalling the pains he used to have. Jamie had the record player turned too high, his thin, taut little body rocking from one foot to the other while he kept his hands pressed over his ears. Brian drew stick figures representing the stars he'd watched on television panel shows the night before, keeping up a low barrage of commercials all the while. He carefully drew a box around each figure, as though to keep it isolated, separate from the rest. Television was

Brian's link with people. Encased in the glass box
of the TV screen, they were far enough away so
that they weren't frightening.

When Brian had come to the school four years
before, his speech was incoherent and he refused
all food, both at home and at school, except for
milk and saltines. But there had always been a
sweetness about him as well as curiosity and intelligence, and these qualities had brought him a
long way. He too had been in my class from the
beginning. I knew how threatening Hannah's anger must be.

All this tension and no Hannah. Where was
she? It was almost ten o'clock. Had she gone back
to Ellen's room? Climbed back inside the jungle
gym? Had she or her mother given up after yesterday? Would that one day be her only day with
us?

Come on, Hannah, I thought. Don't give up before we've even started. It was going to be hard,
but she had so much potential. It was all there—in
her records, in her eyes. It just had to be tapped.
Yesterday I'd almost resented her; now I was impatient for her.

Just then something caught my eye outside the
window. Hannah? I couldn't believe it. She stood
absolutely still about an inch away from the glass.
Her face was turned sidewise, obsured by her
long, matted, gum-filled hair. I tried to watch her
without moving my own head. I had the feeling
she would bolt if she knew she had been seen.
But she was there, that was what counted. She

had come back, she remembered where our room was, and she cared enough to watch us through the window.

Then Brian saw her too and one hand fluttered against his side while he pointed with the other. "Look. There's the girl. She's looking in the window."

Rufus and Jamie turned and Hannah vanished. I ran across the room to our door, opened it, and stepped out, but there was no sign of her. Not in the bushes, not on the driveway. I came back and called to the boys, "Maybe Hannah's in the office. I'll—"

But before I could finish my sentence the hall door opened and there stood Hannah.

Fat, face and hands dirtier than ever, but balancing lightly, almost airily, she stood on her toes in our doorway, clutching a crumpled paper bag.

"Good morning, Hannah," I said. "Come in."

She stood for one moment more and then, half running, half dancing across the few feet to the back of the classroom, she pulled open the closet doors. She stood once more, absolutely still, and then sank slowly to the floor. We were all staring at her. She was an absurd figure with her long dress and matted hair and yet she had an indefinable grace that contrasted with her heavy body and bruised eyes.

I spoke a little louder than usual to break whatever spell was in the room. "I'm glad you're here, Hannah."

Hannah sat without speaking, half in, half out

of the closet. I suddenly realized that it was she who was in total command of the class. This was no way to begin.

I moved toward the door. "Turn off the record player, please, Jamie. Okay, Brian, Hannah. Rufus, get the lights, please. We're going next door to Patty's room for Circle."

Hannah, of course, sat without moving, but the boys moved quickly out the door and down the hall.

I waited one more minute to see if Hannah would change her mind. Nothing. Only her eyes flickered, alert, wary, watching me. Her face and neck were grimy, the pink wads of gum were still in her hair, but her dress was clean. It was the same shapeless style, tied at the waist with a string, but clean. I left Hannah in the closet and walked down the hall after the boys. A clean dress. Somebody cared about Hannah.

The coat closet became Hannah's place in our room. She sat there most of the first two weeks. She had her own cupboard, her own table and chair, even her own work folder, but she barely touched them. In the beginning her grief and anger and confusion were too large to let her work. The most important thing just then, more important than work or discipline, was to let her know that we accepted her.

Children can't begin to learn until they feel safe, and they can't feel safe until they are honestly and completely accepted. A child like Hannah—hospitalized at six weeks, shut in closets, locked out of her home, beaten by both her brother and her father, rejected by the public school—not only feared other people, she feared herself as well.

Hannah knew she was different; she knew that parts of her were frightening, both to herself and others. But she didn't know how to change. She couldn't cut herself in pieces, divide herself in two, bring in only the good part. She needed to know that she was welcome, all of her, the good and the bad. That was enough for now. Changes could come later.

Hannah seemed to understand some of this, and gradually she became more peaceful. Each morning she left her bus and came through the Director's office, down the hall, and into our classroom, closing the hall door behind her. She hung her sweater on the hook beneath her name and then settled herself in the closet to watch the boys arrive. She never greeted me, but she watched Rufus, Jamie, and Brian as they called to each other or exchanged a hug with me. The boys invariably left our doors open and Hannah would get up each time and carefully, softly, close them again. It was as if she realized that she was safe in our room.

Although she didn't participate, she watched us closely. There is no better teacher than another child. As Hannah watched the others, I knew the time would come when she would begin trying to do herself what she had seen the boys do.

Hannah was learning although she never opened

her work folder. She began to touch it more often, going to her cupboard to run her finger across the name I had printed above it and taking out her folder, her paint smock, her book and notebook. None of them were ever used, but still they were hers. She would hold them in her lap and then put them carefully away and return to her seat in the coat closet. She was learning the details of our lives.

Details and routine. Outside of school I never planned ahead, avoiding ruts as much as possible. In school, however, our routine was the same each day. In the topsy-turvy world of emotionally disturbed children, routine provides security. The sameness of each day made it easier for them to cope.

The children arrived at nine o'clock and the first half hour was one of the most important of the day, although it might not seem so to an uninformed eye. Crises of the night before exploded in the classroom, and it was important for the teacher to be there to comfort or control. Treasures were brought in, and the teacher had to be there to share the pleasure of each small discovery. Sometimes problems arose on the way to school, or a child arrived without breakfast and the teacher needed to go down to the refrigerator in the furnace room for the milk and cereal that were always kept there. Although our children were not primarily underprivileged, often there was so much chaos in their homes that breakfast was impossible.

By nine thirty most personal crises had been dealt with and we were ready for the larger world of Circle. Circle was a kind of morning assembly where the whole school gathered together. At least we had until this year. Now we were too many for one room, and so the Director had divided us into two groups, the older children in one, the younger children in the other. During this time there was singing and dancing and group games. The purpose was threefold: to help the children relate and participate in a group, to improve gross motor coordination, and also to give the teachers the opportunity to see the other children in the school. At staff meetings on Wednesdays we discussed everyone, and it was necessary that we have at least a surface knowledge of each child.

After Circle, the children went to the bathroom and then came back to their classrooms. For the rest of the day, each teacher had a special program for each child.

In our room we started with the Best and the Worst. In searching for ways to help the children learn to communicate, I had discovered Best and Worst. Most of our children had grave difficulty with communication. Some couldn't talk at all; some were elective mutes, able to talk but refusing to do so; some, like Rufus, were too verbose; some articulated clearly but without meaning. Because communication is so important, I worked hard at finding ways to involve the children.

"Show and Tell" didn't work. Our children had

little to show and nothing to tell. To get through to them it was necessary to turn up the volume and intensity of communication.

A question like "Tell me what you did yesterday" didn't bring any response; it was too general, too vague. But when each and every day I asked them to report on the Best Thing and the Worst Thing that had happened to them, they not only responded, they began to savor the opportunity. Like most ideas, this started small and grew. When I had first asked the question four years before, answers had been a word or two at the most. But I insisted they all have a chance, whether they used it or not, and gradually they all began to talk a bit and—more amazing still—to listen to each other.

There were different children then—only Brian still remained of that first group—but each day we talked a little more until it became necessary to have limits, so that no one child could monopolize the time. Then, because the world of fantasy was so vivid—even more so than to other children, and therefore less distinct from reality—the Best Thing became their wishes, the Worst their dreams. This, of course, was good—so good and so surprising that the school psychiatrist who visited our class shook his head in amazement as he heard children labeled "schizophrenic" or "autistic" talk and listen to each other.

But it wasn't enough simply to get the children to talk. I wanted them to understand the difference between reality and fantasy. It seemed to me that if they were ever to travel all the way back to live in the world, they needed to know and be able to differentiate between the two. So there got to be two parts to Best and Worst, "real" and "pretend," and the children sternly reminded each other of this. If a child began to talk about trucks as though they were people, calling the headlights "eyes," another child was sure to remind him, "First the real, then the pretend."

So Best and Worst became a part of my teaching equipment, and today, as usual, we pushed tables together, directly after Circle, all of us eager to begin. In order to have time for reading, language arts, and math, and then to go outside or play before lunch, each child was only allowed five minutes—but to me it was one of the most important parts of the day.

After lunch there was a rest period, then art, science, films, playground, and auditory and visual motor training. The afternoon went by even more quickly than the morning. The day was too short; there was never enough time to do all that I had hoped to do.

During those first two weeks I made no demands on Hannah, letting her absorb the details and atmosphere of the school, letting the boys grow used to her, letting peace and a semblance of tranquillity return to the class. Her despair no longer seeped constantly into our room, corroding the warm safety. As long as I asked nothing of Hannah she was quiet, sitting half in, half out of the closet, eating out of her paper bag when she felt like it, watching us all the time.

But this interlude was almost over. Mrs. Rosnic was scheduled to come in to see me the third Monday after school started. I felt that after that I could begin to ask more of Hannah.

4

Hannah's mother came heavily, hesitantly, into our classroom. She was a large woman dressed in a cotton housedress just like Hannah's, although hers reached only to her knees and was covered with a dark cloth coat.

I had telephoned Mrs. Rosnic at the end of that first day to ask if she could come in for a conference. Although she was hesitant and it had taken two weeks, she was here and I was grateful. Helping Hannah was not going to be easy. She was going to have to give up old established ways and learn new ones. There were difficult weeks ahead, and before I initiated any major changes at school I wanted to talk to Hannah's mother and learn what Hannah was like at home. I needed to fill in the gaps left by the psychological reports, to find out what sort of relationship there was between Hannah and her brother and sister, between Hannah and her mother. Our school day was only five and a half hours long. There were eighteen and a half other hours I wanted to know about.

I had been sitting at one of the low tables, but as Mrs. Rosnic hesitated in the doorway I got up and walked toward her. "Please come in."

But she remained where she was, her eyes moving rapidly around the room. By now the boys' papers and drawings covered one wall. We had begun a large mural on another, but the only sign of Hannah was her name on her cubby and above the coat hook in the closet.

"May I take your coat?" I asked.

For the first time Mrs. Rosnic looked directly at me and it was my turn to stop, startled by the fear in her eyes.

As gently as I could, I took her coat and hung it in the closet beside my own light sweater, and then, impulsively, I moved them both so that they hung together on Hannah's own hook. I came back and sat down at the round wooden table. "Thank you for coming in," I said. "I know how difficult it must be for you to get away with the three children at home, but I wanted to talk to you a little bit about Hannah. I'm happy to have her in my class this year."

Mrs. Rosnic came across the room then, stopping in front of me. "You not getting rid of her?"

So that was the fear; it was still there in her chopped, guttural speech. There were traces of an accent. I must remember to check and see what language was spoken in the home. It was possible that much of Hannah's garbled speech was a poor imitation of the words she heard exchanged between her mother and grandfather. But that could come later.

Now I had to get through that fear, let Mrs. Rosnic know that I didn't want to get rid of Hannah. On the contrary, what I wanted was to get closer, know more. The best way I knew was to say it simply and straight.

"I won't get rid of Hannah," I promised. "She'll be here in this class all year."

Mrs. Rosnic sat down opposite me then, her eyes never leaving my face. "In other school, every time they called me for conference, they warn Hannah is too bad. They say she have to go."

"Not here. When I call you, it's because I want to know more, try to figure out how to help more."

Mrs. Rosnic drew in her breath and then let it out in a long slow sigh, but as her body relaxed, more of her weariness showed. "Ah, she is so hard, that one. I don't know what to do with her. Yelling, screaming half the time. Most other time she just sit, dumb, do nothing. Once in while she play joke. Put mouse in Grandpa's bed and laugh and laugh when he yell."

I tried to picture the house. I knew Grandpa lived downstairs, but where would Hannah get a mouse?

"A real mouse?" I asked.

"Lots of mice around. They're not trouble. Hannah like them. The cats are good, get rid of most of mice. Only if rats come, then the cats scared."

"Mrs. Rosnic, Hannah doesn't talk to us here at school. Does she talk at home?"

"She not talk Carl or Grandpa, but sometime she talk to me. Say yes, no, other words. Grandpa say she not make sense, but I know what she mean."

It was hard to tell from this whether Hannah spoke more or whether Mrs. Rosnic's interpretations were better.

"Listen," I said. "What's Hannah like in other ways at home? I know she goes to the bathroom by herself. Does she also wash, brush her teeth, dress herself?"

"No." Mrs. Rosnic's sighs were deep now. "She never wash. She sleep in dress all night. Won't get out of it. Next morning Carl or Grandpa hold her and I get other dress on her."

"Carl. Does Hannah play with him or with her sister?"

"Play? Nobody play. Just fight, fight, fight. At each other day and night. Carl tease her all the time. Now he tell her she going to retard school and she cry and cry."

I felt like crying myself. Poverty, dirt, ridicule. I looked away for a minute, trying to clear my mind, to see what to do next. I turned back to Mrs. Rosnic. "What about friends? Does Hannah play with other children on the block?"

Mrs. Rosnic sat up straight, definite now. "I careful with her. Keep her in back yard so neighbor kids not make fun. Sometime when I fixing Grandpa's food she get away, but not much. Mostly I keep her near." A wistful look came over Mrs. Rosnic's face. "Sometime I wish ... I think how good if she could help some. You know. Like set table. Maybe even dry dishes."

I reached across the table. If she had been a child I would have touched her then, but instead

I touched the water glass of the roses and left my hand out open on the table.

"I know I wish too much," she continued. "Should be glad she not worse. Grandpa say she can't be worse, say she better dead from operation. But I don't know. It nice, kind of, you know—to have somebody like me."

My heart ached and angered all at the same time, even more than when I'd read the reports. No wonder this good, uneducated woman was close to giving up. Under the weariness and despair had there once been laughter and other dreams? It was too late now to recover those dreams; too late for Grandpa and maybe for Mrs. Rosnic. But not for Hannah. Maybe I couldn't do anything about the poverty or the loneliness, or Carl or baby Helen, but I could help Hannah. And so could Mrs. Rosnic.

"Listen," I said. "You're not expecting too much at all. You're exactly right. Hannah should be learning to help you around the house. She can learn to do all those things. And more. Much more."

Mrs. Rosnic looked at me and then fished in her large black pocketbook for a handerchief. I got up and brought back a box of Kleenex from the counter and set it down hard on the table.

"Hannah can learn to wash and dress herself and help you with the housework. And she can learn to read and write."

This was too much. I had gone too far. Mrs.

Rosnic shook her head at me. "No," she said. "You don't know. Grandpa say she moron."

"I do know and Grandpa's wrong," I insisted. "I have known other children as troubled as Hannah. I have read her records and I have watched her here in the classroom. I don't believe she's retarded. I believe she's able to learn and grow and do a great deal more than she ever has."

Mrs. Rosnic looked at me directly, challenging. "Why you care? Why you want to do this?"

It was a fair, honest question and I wished that I could answer. But I had never been able to find words for the way I felt. I could talk easily about the children, or to the children, but when it came to describing my own feelings, I was inarticulate. Perhaps the words imprisoned in the children spoke to something locked inside me. I tried to soften my silence with a smile so that it wouldn't seem a rebuff. "I don't know," I answered as honestly as I could. "I wish I could put it into words. I can't explain, but I hope you'll trust me."

I went to the coat closet and got Mrs. Rosnic's coat and my sweater from Hannah's hook and then held the coat for her. Mrs. Rosnic stood facing me, still looking at me. Finally she turned and put one arm into a sleeve. "Ah, well, never mind. Words come hard. I know. And anyway, the ones that say them so easy—well, I hear plenty of words before." She put the second arm in.

"It's not going to be easy with Hannah," I said. "That's one thing for sure. It's going to mean a lot of work for both of us, and it will be harder for you because you're with her more. Sometimes you're going to have to be very strong. Hannah's been used to having her own way, and she's not going to be able to all the time now. She won't like it, and sometimes she's going to get very angry with both of us."

I shrugged on my sweater and then was caught by surprise as Mrs. Rosnic reached out and smoothed it across my shoulders. Her fingers were rough and they snagged on the soft wool, but her hand itself was strong and warm. "Listen. It okay. I tell Grandpa. It okay. Hannah, she lucky this year."

5

The next morning after Circle I went and sat on the floor in the closet next to Hannah. The period of research was over. I had learned all I could from outside sources. Now it was up to me. I set my goals for Hannah. They might change, but I had to have something to aim for.

The first thing I had to do was get Hannah out of the coat closet. Observation has its values, but it was time for her to move closer, become part of us. "Listen," I said. "I want you to come and sit with us during Best and Worst today. You don't have to talk, but I want you at the table. You're part of our class and I want you with us."

Hannah pulled her long dress over her head.

I pulled the dress down and spoke directly into her face. "If you can come by yourself, fine. If not, I'll help you."

I wanted her to understand that this was not a question of choice. She didn't have to decide anything. I had made the decision. She had sat in the closet for two weeks. That was long enough.

I hesitated for a minute. The trick was to know when to ask for more and when to stop. Each step like this was a risk, the line between success and failure is so small. I had thought carefully about when and where to begin with Hannah, and now I decided to go ahead. This was the time, right after Circle. She was fascinated by Best and Worst. I had seen her looking, listening, from the closet. And contradictory though it seems, I knew that the first move is sometimes easier if someone else insists on it. I insisted now. I stood up. "Okay, Hannah. Let's go."

She pulled the dress back over her head.

I reached under the dress, found her hand, and pulled her to her feet. Caught by surprise, she came up easily but let out a howl of rage.

"This morning you're going to sit with us. This morning and every other morning from now on. You're part of our class."

Standing beside me, Hannah braced her feet like a balky mule and pulled hard to get away.

The classroom was large, over forty feet long. The boys had set up the table in the middle of the room and they sat there now, watching us. We had about twenty feet to go to reach the table. I was sure I could manage that. Hannah was husky, but I had a lot of inches, pounds, and years in my favor and my will was as strong as her own.

"If you can control yourself, Hannah, great. If not, I'll help you control yourself."

I started walking toward the table, holding her hand tightly in my own and propelling her along with me.

Her howling ceased. She planted both feet close together again and braked us to a stop and smashed her foot—*crack!* into my ankle. I yelped in surprise, but I caught her foot in time and pulled off first one shoe and then the other. She could kick all she wanted now.

I had been through this many times before. Other children in other years had kicked and bitten, but they had gentled. We had all survived, and eventually they had made it back to public school.

The howling began again, but there was little she could do, and more in sorrow than in anger Hannah allowed herself to be pulled to the table.

"Get another chair, please, Bri."

I sat Hannah down next to me and said to the boys, "Whose turn is it to begin Best and Worst today?"

My eyes, my attention, were focused on the boys. I kept a steady grip on Hannah's hand, but that was all. Except for this hold on her hand, we ignored her. She alternately cried and yelled for the half hour. She was loud, but we were louder and managed to hear each other.

At the end of the half hour, the boys went to get their work folders from their cupboards. I looked down at Hannah's tear-stained face. "Thank you, babe, for being with us." Then I released her hand.

For one brief moment she looked at me and then raced back to her closet seat. Her scuffed brown shoes still lay on the floor. I took them to her and then went back to help the boys with their reading. All the rest of the morning she sat there watching us, not saying anything, not yelling, just sitting there holding her shoes in her lap.

At the end of the morning I sent the boys out for recess with another class. The tension in the room had been hard on them, though none of them had mentioned it and they had worked well all morning. Still, they needed to get outside to run, to throw, to yell a little. At the same time I didn't want to leave Hannah. It was important that she know that I wanted to be with her. There is a great difference between someone arbitrarily imposing demands on you and someone working through a difficult situation with you. I wanted Hannah to know that, whatever I asked of her, she wouldn't have to do it alone.

I needed something more, something to hook her interest, make her forget herself. I wanted to capture Hannah, lure her, not force her again. Suddenly I remembered the doll family.

I had ordered the dolls from the school supply catalog the year before and stored them in my closet, waiting for the right time to bring them out. Surely, if there was a right time, this was it.

The next morning, after Circle, I announced that we were going to add something new to Best and Worst. I placed the box in the middle of the table. In the closet I said to Hannah, "Hey, come see. I've got a box for you to open."

She peeked out of the closet to see what I was talking about. The box sat invitingly on the table. Hannah couldn't resist it. She skirted the table twice on her own and then suddenly sat down and peeled off the tape and pulled the box open. She lifted out the brown crumpled packing paper and sat staring at the contents. Then, one by one, she lifted out the members of the miniature family, unwrapping each one carefully and laying it on the table. Man, woman, girl, boy, baby.

The dolls were made of a hard, waxlike substance, a kind of molded rubber, pliable, durable, sturdy enough to take bending and pounding.

We all sat looking at the dolls. No one seemed sure what to do next. On impulse, I picked up the woman and girl dolls and put their arms around each other. "My best thing is that Elizabeth came home from college for a visit last night."

I talked for about two minutes, telling how my daughter and I had gone to a movie and bought some ice cream. As I talked I was bending the dolls to sit, pushing them along the table, pretending they were moving in the car.

The children watched, their eyes never moving from the little figures. When I finished I laid the two dolls back on the table.

Rufus was sitting next to me, and he picked up

the man doll and in a loud, authoritarian voice said, "If I'm doing the cooking, I'll do it the way I want to. So *shut up!*"

We all stared at him. None of us had ever heard Rufus speak like that before. Obviously he was being someone else.

Now he picked up the woman doll and in a high, wistful voice said, "You never listen to me, no matter what it is. Cooking or anything else."

Maybe not, but we listened to Rufus. Forgetting time limits, we sat spellbound as he acted out a household drama, using first one doll and then another. When he finished he pushed the dolls to the middle of the table and leaned back with a tired, satisfied sigh.

Jamie picked up each doll and inspected it carefully. He petted the baby and kissed the mother and then put them back without saying a word.

Brian had his turn and acted out a TV commercial.

And now, look at Hannah. She picked up the boy doll and put him under the box. She pushed hard on the box, which wobbled in an unsatisfactory way. She got up from the table, went to the block wagon, and pulled it back to the table. What was she doing? She laid out one, two, three, four blocks in a square and put the boy doll in the middle. Was he supposed to be her brother, Carl? *Bang*, she put a block on the top, then another and another.

Hannah looked up at us and smiled. For the first time in our room she smiled with pure joy, as she added block after block on top of the boy doll.

6

Hannah came to Best and Worst each day, but she still ate in the closet. She brought her lunch in a crumpled brown paper bag and tucked it safely behind her coat every morning. Then, all day, she ate whenever she was hungry, sitting on the floor in the closet.

She ate like an animal, tearing at the food with her teeth, no matter how soft it might be. She aimed for the center of the cupcake, trying for the choicest morsel, eyes glancing right and left, on the lookout even while she ate. Once she had made contact with the food, her fingers rapidly prodded as much as possible into her mouth. Then, when she couldn't fit any more in, she clamped her teeth together, cutting off the rest. The crust, the cheese, the jelly, the crumbs, fell to her lap or the floor. But even these she guarded carefully and ate when she felt hungry again.

It was a sad and terrible way to eat. I'd let it continue in those beginning weeks because I had to know Hannah. I watched, listened, learned her behavior. I couldn't begin to teach until I knew where to start.

I knew Hannah now, not intimately yet, but

enough to realize that it was worth the long struggle ahead. The intellect, the curiosity, the potential were there and so was the motivation. Food was extremely important to her. In the area of food, I would have Hannah's complete attention.

I waited one more week; then I stopped Hannah as she arrived and quickly, before she could react, took the paper lunch bag out of her hands. I placed it in full view but high above her head, on the closet shelf.

As I took her lunch bag away Hannah drew back, mobilized for action. She raced for the closet, jumping, leaping, trying to reach the paper bag that I'd put on the shelf. But this lasted only a few seconds. Almost immediately she ran back to get a chair. Inwardly, I exulted at her reaction, her immediate understanding of the problem, her swift attempt at a new solution. Outwardly, I took the chair away and said, "Not today, Hannah. Today you're going to eat with us."

Fury exploded in our room. She understood what I said and she was not about to let it happen. She ran for another chair, and another, and another, as I blocked her attempts. Finally frustration and anger caught up and she went down on the floor in the knee-chest position of the first day. Once again she drove her head down toward the hard tile floor, howling all the while.

I sat down beside her. "Hannah. Nobody's going to take your lunch. It's yours. I'm going to keep it for you on the shelf until lunchtime. We eat lunch at twelve. Look, see the clock? When both hands are up at the top, we'll eat."

Again she couldn't resist. The rocking stopped and for a second she allowed herself one swift look at the clock above the door. She understood me; she had receptive language, and she knew what a clock was!

But the pause was only for an instant. Back to the rocking. And it was only nine thirty. I couldn't keep taking chairs away all morning. What to do for two and a half hours, with three other children to teach?

I sat beside Hannah, thinking, looking around the room. Finally I spotted a pipe running along the ceiling inside the closet. There might be just enough room to prop her lunch there. It would still be visible, in plain sight, so she would know it was safe, but there was no chair in the room high enough to let Hannah reach it.

I got up and moved the lunch bag. By standing on a chair I could just reach the pipe, and I wedged Hannah's lunch behind it. She grabbed a chair and ran with it to the closet, but the chair was no help this time; I was a good foot and a half taller than Hannah. As soon as she realized this, she pushed the chair over and came after me. Yelling, screaming, her hands clawed at me.

I put my arms around her and held her from behind. "Hannah, Hannah. You are so foolish. All this fuss about your lunch. Nobody will take it, I promise you. Nobody can get it, except me, and I'll give it to you at lunchtime. Twelve o'clock, when both hands are at the top of the clock. You watch. You'll see." Hannah broke away from me and ran back to the chairs.

Brian and Rufus were both trying to work, but their eyes never left Hannah for long. Finally Rufus took his book and lay in a spot on the floor just behind the free-standing bookcases. He read out loud, talking to himself at the end of each line—"Don't worry, Rufus, that ol' dummy girl will go home soon"—or sometimes just "It's all right. Don't be scared, Rufus." It's not surprising that he barely finished a page.

Brian had even more difficulty handling the situation. He abandoned his book altogether and went back to his old-time pacing of perimeters. He no longer ran or croaked out strangled cries, nor did his arms flap wildly, as they had when he had first come to school. Now he walked silently around the edges of our room and only his fingertips trembled against his sides.

But Jamie couldn't stand it. His own need for security was so desperate, his ability to cope with feelings so minimal, that when Hannah exploded he replied in kind. As she pushed chairs over in the back of the room, he pushed them against the side walls, grabbing one and pounding it up and down.

But as the minutes dragged on Hannah quieted a little and Jamie calmed too. I crouched down beside him and gathered him up, holding him close, murmuring against his neck, "Jamie, Jamie, I'm sorry. I know it's hard. Now just hang in, okay? Just stay with us. It'll get better. This is the worst. It will be better."

I knew he really didn't understand all I said, but it didn't matter. Our language depended more on tones and touch than words. I needed to know that he wouldn't revert back to the desperate runaway of the year before, circling the church and dashing toward the highway. Jamie needed to know that the strange noisy girl had not usurped his place.

This was Jamie's second year with me. He had been at the school for two years and had spent most of his first year running, with his young, bewildered teacher always just a little too far behind. Then he'd been assigned to me. I suspected that Jamie was retarded, at least to some degree. While the school was designed for seriously emotionally disturbed children, it is often difficult to distinguish between autism and retardation. When a child doesn't respond, it is sometimes hard to tell whether this is because he refuses or is unable.

With Jamie, it was possible that autism and retardation were both present or that, as some professionals think, the two are intertwined. In any event, I asked for what I thought he was capable of doing and rejoiced in his small successes.

I sighed as I held Jamie, listening to Rufus muttering behind me, watching Brian pause at the chalkboard and nervously begin to draw the panel of stars from the telethon of the night before. So much time was being lost, time I needed to keep Jamie steady, let Rufus grow, help Brian make it to public school. And yet there was no other way. Hannah had to become part of us, had to find her own place within the accepted limits of the class. It was up to me as teacher to somehow get her there.

I looked at Hannah over the top of Jamie's head. She was still in the closet, trying to balance one chair on top of another. At least she was off the floor working on the problem. I turned back to Jamie as he wiggled around in my lap and put his hands across my eyes. Close relationships have their own rituals, and I knew what to say. "Where are you, Jamie? Where'd you go? I can't see you any place." Down came his hands. "Oh, there you are! Boy, am I glad to see you!" And the fact that he nuzzled in close announced the success of our old foolish game.

Within a half hour Hannah had given up hope of reaching her lunch and had decided to keep watch instead. She turned one of the small chairs to face the closet, and for the next hour and a half she sat with her back to the rest of the room and her eyes on her lunch, or occasionally on the clock.

With Hannah quiet, some peace returned to the room. Gradually, the boys drifted back to their desks or one of the round tables, going from time to time to check on their work schedules or to get new books from their cubbies. Each day I made up a new schedule for each child and taped it to the counter above his cubby. I tried to list each task, each separate page that was to be done that day, so that as they finished a page or particular assignment they could cross it off and immediately see what to do next. This gave them satisfaction in the accomplishment and a structured, constructive way to move around.

By eleven forty-five an amazing amount had been accomplished, and the boys put their things away and went to get washed for lunch. Hannah obviously wasn't going to move. There wasn't a chance that she would leave that lunch bag. Although her hands and face were as dirty as ever, washing seemed like a matter of small importance compared to what lay ahead: I was going to have to get that paper bag from behind the pipe and then take it down to Patty's room, the same room where we had Circle.

I skipped washing myself and sat with Hannah while the boys were gone. She paid absolutely no attention to me. I sat beside her in a chair the same size as hers, but she didn't turn her head a fraction of an inch. We both silently stared at the crumpled paper bag, which now seemed enormous in size. Better tell Hannah what was going to happen. If she was like me, she would like to be prepared ahead of time.

"At twelve o'clock I'm going to get down your lunch and take it to Patty's room so that you can eat with us today. No more alone in the closet. Okay?"

Not a flicker.

I decided to be optimistic. "Okay. Good. That's all set, then."

I knew what I was going to do. I was going to cut whatever sandwich there was in the bag into four small squares and let Hannah eat them one at a time, while we ate with her.

Ate with her? Eat with her? I sat up straight. How could I be so stupid? She'd need somebody to show her how, somebody to eat a sandwich with her. I didn't have a sandwich. Neither did the boys. Zoe, our secretary, warmed a donated casserole each day for the school lunch, and we all ate that together. But to ask Hannah to give up her lunch and eat casserole was no fair. I'd promised her that sandwich.

I glanced at the clock at the same time Hannah did, and our eyes brushed for a second. Eleven fifty-five. I got up and walked as quietly as I could to the door, not wanting to set off any vibrations. "Be back in just a minute."

Hannah rose in protest.

"Really. I'll be back by twelve o'clock. Just have to do something for a second."

Down the hall, into the furnace room. Somewhere in the refrigerator was a jar of peanut butter that we kept for emergencies. Okay. Now bread. No bread. . . . Oh, there it is, in the vegetable drawer. Now a knife. Good. Okay. No time to make a sandwich now.

I trotted back to our room, opened the door slowly, took a chair, and went straight to the closet and pried Hannah's lunch from behind the pipe.

I headed quickly for the door again. "Lunchtime. Let's go."

I looked at the clock as I went out the door. Twelve o'clock on the dot.

I was halfway to Patty's room, walking fast, before Hannah caught up to me. She was mad and she wanted her lunch. I didn't blame her. On the other hand, if I gave it to her now, I knew what would happen. She would turn and run back to the classroom and gobble her sandwich in the closet.

Peanut butter under my left armpit, bread and knife in my left hand, right hand holding Hannah's lunch bag high above my head, my walk turned to a trot.

"We're going to have a great lunch. All ready in just a minute. Whoops."

I almost lost the peanut butter as Hannah wound her arms around my legs and sat down on my feet.

But we were almost there. I shuffled along with Hannah on my feet. I could see heads watching from doors and I felt like a football player going for the last yard before the touchdown.

Brian had the door open, and once inside I took advantage of the surprise of new surroundings. There were four girls in Patty's class and all of them crowded around and peered down at Hannah, who was being propelled into the room on my feet. Wanda Gomez, a dark, heavy girl, touched Hannah's head before she bit her own arm. "No legs. Girl's got no legs. Poor girl."

Hannah loosened her grasp in surprise for one second and I slid my feet out from under her, raced for the piano in the back of the room, and dumped the contents of Hannah's lunch bag on the piano top. Sandwich in waxed paper and a chocolate cupcake. I ripped open the wrapper and, with my silver knife, sliced the jelly sandwich into four inaccurate rectangles. Next the cupcake. Then everything back into the paper bag, except one small square of sandwich.

Patty had already set the table, and I sat down at one end and put the square inch of sandwich on the paper plate next to mine. The peanut butter and loaf of bread I put on my plate. Hannah's bag between my feet. Ahhh! Made it. I looked up for Hannah.

She was on the other side of the table, staring at me.

"Come on, lovey," I said. "Time for lunch. See, this is how we do it here. A little at a time. Come on now. Sit here with me."

I began working on my own sandwich. Hannah came slowly now, not pushing, not clawing. She stood beside me, watching as I spread the cold, clumpy peanut butter on the bread and put another piece of bread on top. Deliberately, I cut my own sandwich into pieces the same size as hers.

Hannah still hesitated beside me. I pulled out her chair, silently urging her toward me, and picked up my own small square of sandwich. I tipped the sandwich toward her in a friendly gesture and then put it in my mouth, bit it in half, and put the other half back on the plate.

Suddenly Hannah sat down, picked up her quarter of sandwich, and put it in her mouth. She didn't bite it in half, but who cared? Refinements could come later. No crusts or jelly were slobbering down her chin; she was out of the closet, sitting at a table, eating with us. I smiled at her around the cold peanut butter stuck to the roof of my mouth and served us each another square of sandwich.

It was Brian rather than Rufus who first began to move toward Hannah. He was fascinated by her eating, as I should have known he would be.

Brian had had his own eating problems, far more severe than Hannah's. When he had first come to school four years before, his entire diet had consisted of chocolate milk and saltines. We didn't know why—though his parents suspected abuse at a child care center—but Brian had not begun to eat other foods until almost a year after he first came to school. We tried numerous means and methods until finally, in the end, we had forced his first bite and he began to eat. This had proved—to me, at least—not that it is right to force a child to eat but that almost anything can become a learning experience if there is enough caring involved.

Brian now ate normally and well, but Hannah's

struggles must have stirred all kinds of memories, and his fascination with her eating was understandable. He began to sit on her other side at lunchtime. He did it quietly, without comment, simply moving in and occupying the seat next to her.

Gradually Hannah's fears calmed, and by the end of the week she knew what to expect. Each day at noon I lifted down her paper bag and took it to Patty's room, where I cut her sandwich into squares and gave them to her. Each day as we walked to lunch together I continued to carry her paper lunch bag and my own sandwich. Each day was the same; each day I did as I had promised.

One day in the middle of the following week, I took Hannah's sandwich from behind the pipe and my foil-wrapped sandwich from my purse and gave them both to Hannah to carry.

Her eyes widened as I handed them to her. She stood very, very still, looking first at me and then at our sandwiches.

I waited. I had given her the sandwiches because I wanted her to know that I trusted her, and trust is something better explained by actions than words. There's no sure way to know when to trust, but I thought Hannah was ready and I wanted to give her the option: she could run, she could bolt back to the closet with our sandwiches, or she could walk with me, carrying our lunch.

She took her paper bag in one hand and my sandwich in the other and started down the hall. I walked slowly after her. Then abruptly she stopped and turned around, heading back the way she'd come. Had I guessed wrong, acted too soon? Was she off to the closet?

She stopped when she reached me and stepped in front of me, forcing me to stop as well. Then, with her head bent down, never looking at me, she opened the paper bag and dropped my sandwich in with hers. Still not looking up, she reached out for my hand with her free one and we walked down the hall together, while my heart boomed with such excitement that I could feel it in my head.

Days pass like minutes in a school like ours where each child is such a fascinating, intricate individual. At lunch a few days later, I suddenly saw Hannah reach out and grab a handful of Brian's spaghetti. I grabbed too, covering her hand with mine, prying open her fingers so that the spaghetti fell back on his plate and both our hands were covered with the red, sticky sauce.

"No, Hannah. Not that way. You eat spaghetti with a fork."

But Brian knew better. Quickly he dumped some of his own spaghetti onto Hannah's plate and chopped at it with his fork, trying to cut the spaghetti into pieces small enough to stay in a spoon.

"Help her, Mary. Help Hannah eat the spaghetti."

He pushed his spoon toward me and I picked it up, put it between Hannah's greasy fingers, and put my own hand over hers, guiding the spoon down into the food.

Brian began to eat rapidly from his plate with his fork, so excited that his thin, wiry little body bounced off his chair after every two or three bites.

I felt Hannah's fingers tense under my hand and gradually I relaxed my own fingers. She was holding the spoon by herself now. Then, her eyes on Brian, she began to eat.

I called Mrs. Rosnic immediately after lunch, unable to wait till school was over. I told her what had happened and asked her not to send lunch any more. From now on Hannah would eat whatever we did. No longer would she sit in the closet eating her solitary sandwich; no longer would she have special food. From now on she would sit at the table with us and share our meal. She was one of us and we would eat together.

7

Those next few weeks, the middle weeks of October, flew by and Hannah flew with them. She was out of the closet most of the time now, literally dancing around our classroom, touching, turning, examining everything in the room while the rest of us watched and still tried to do our work. Still not speaking, still in the long cotton housedress, yet she was entrancing. Somehow Hannah was getting prettier. She was cleaner, for one thing. As the layers of grime came off, it was possible to see her fine creamy skin.

Since Hannah was eating with us now it was fair to expect her to wash—or perhaps it is more accurate to say "be washed." Each day before lunch I filled the bathroom sink with warm water and washed her hands and face. At first I had washed only her hands, using a thin washcloth because it wasn't as hard or slippery or scary as soap and also because I could gradually move the washcloth to her neck, her face.

I called Mrs. Rosnic again to report this and to urge her to try the same thing before supper. She agreed to try and added that yes, she thought

Hannah was doing a little better, but her voice seemed sad. When I asked if anything was wrong, she said that the baby had a cold and that she thought maybe she was getting it.

Two days later when I was washing Hannah's face, she whimpered and pulled away and I saw that under her matted, dirty, reddish hair, which I still hadn't touched, her right ear was covered with a thick yellow crust.

I took Hannah to the office at once. We didn't have a doctor at school (or rather, the only doctor on our staff was the psychiatrist), but Dianne, one of our teachers, was a registered nurse and the Director called her down to the office to look at Hannah. She confirmed what we had suspected and the Director telephoned Mrs. Rosnic immediately to tell her that Hannah had a badly infected ear and should be seen by a doctor. I took Hannah back to our room and kept her quiet and close to me for the rest of the day.

Hannah was absent for ten days, and when she came back she acted as though she barely recognized us. She headed straight for the closet, not only sitting there but closing the door except for a tiny crack. She didn't bring her lunch but now, instead of eating, she threw her food or pushed it away.

What was wrong? Was this just the aftermath of illness or had something else happened while she was home? I talked to Mrs. Rosnic, but she couldn't tell me anything, except that the doctor's examination and the ear infection itself had both been very painful. Did Hannah blame me? In her mind had the earache somehow risen out of school? I tried to talk to her a little through the crack in the closet door, but it seemed doubtful that she heard me.

The not knowing is one of the most difficult things about working with nonverbal children: not knowing what goes on when they're away from you, not knowing what goes on in their heads when they're with you.

Regressions weren't new to me. I had seen them many times before and worked them through with other children. After every vacation there was almost always some sort of back-sliding; after an illness there was more. It never was easy. Each tiny step of progress had been gained at such high price that to see it lost, even temporarily, was difficult. But no learning experience is a constant upward climb. There are always peaks, plateaus, and valleys. This wasn't what bothered me about Hannah. It was the anger.

She would have nothing to do with any of us. Everything anyone tried to do was wrong. Even the doll family and Best and Worst failed to bring her out of the closet. We were back where we started, or worse. Again, if it was hard for me, it was harder for the boys. They had been pleased and excited about her progress. There had been a sunny loveliness to Hannah as she explored the room. Sometimes she'd had the air of a clown as she experimented with new materials, imitating one or another of the boys. This was all gone now, and again the added dimension of difficulty for the boys was that this could happen to them. Their own emotional stability was still frail. If Hannah could change so much, it was possible that they could too.

I tried hard all week to regain lost ground with Hannah and at the same time to reassure the boys. Nothing worked very well, and by Friday afternoon I was not only discouraged, I was tired.

Well, there were only a few hours left to the week. I'd just try to get through the afternoon as painlessly as possible. I put a record on and got out paint, paper, brushes. Perhaps painting would give us a respite or a chance to express some feelings. The boys were pleased, and in a little while we were all involved.

Everyone was working on his own thing. Brian was painting the sides of a refrigerator carton to make himself a telephone booth. Jamie was finger-painting on a portion of the floor covered with newspaper, happily moving the wet, bright colors over the slippery paper and himself as well. Rufus didn't know what he felt like doing, and he watched first one and then another. Finally he decided to join me.

I'd taken our pumpkin from the counter, the dried cornstalks from our outside door, and an old yellow pitcher from the furnace room and put them together on a table by the window. There were no oils in school, but I had orange, red, white, yellow, and brown poster paints and I mixed new colors as I needed them. I was no artist, but I loved to sketch and paint. It helped me to see, made me more aware of line and color and reality. I was fascinated by perspective, continually amazed that half of what I saw was supplied by my mind's eye.

Rufus got his own paper and brush, commandeered the orange paint I'd mixed, and began to paint an orange pumpkin. "Can I make a face on it?" he asked. "Even if it doesn't really have a face?"

I glanced at him. "It's your pumpkin. You can do anything you want with it, Ruf."

I had looked away for only a minute. But that minute had been long enough for Hannah to come out of the closet, pick up the red and yellow paint jars, and pour the contents on my paper.

Anger flared inside me and I turned abruptly. "Cut it out, Hannah. What do you think you're doing, anyway? Stop it now. That's enough."

My voice was loud and Jamie burst into tears as Hannah threw the yellow paint jar at me. It shattered against the tile floor by my feet, and my dreams and plans for Hannah seemed to shatter with it.

8

But a paint jar is only a paint jar and never worth a dream. Besides, a teacher's dream dies hard and is easily refurbished, and by Monday morning I had a new plan.

The plan was simply to get out of the classroom. I'd been trying too hard, pushing Hannah too much, attempting to recapture growth, and it didn't work. Hannah herself had put the final period to a poor week's work when she had thrown the paint. We needed to leave the classroom, the work, the mistakes behind us. We needed a fresh start.

For me, Indian summer is one of the loveliest times of year, the best of summer mixed with autumn, and that's what we had that Monday morning: bright Yale-blue October sky with sun shimmering, bouncing off every glossy surface that it struck so that there seemed to be twice as much sunshine. The world shone and the temperature was just right for sweaters and a picnic.

I waited in the parking lot for the children and gathered them into my car as they arrived so that they wouldn't have to relive the incident of Hannah's rage on the previous Friday. Soon everyone was settled in the car—the three boys in the back, Hannah in the front seat beside me.

There had been a slight delay over seat belts, Hannah at first refusing to fasten hers, but now everything was snug and we were off to Thunder Mountain. Sandwiches, lemonade, apples, and cookies were packed in the trunk along with blankets and storybooks.

My own spirits began to rise as we left suburbia behind and drove into farm and orchard country with the mountains just beyond. We sang as we drove. We always sang in the car, and today Rufus began:

> "She'll be comin' round the mountain
>   when she comes (*giddy-ap—whoa!*),
> She'll be comin' round the mountain
>   when she comes . . ."

At least the boys and I sang. Hannah sat silently beside me.

Once Brian leaned forward and said to Hannah, "Why don't you sing, Hannah? Why don't you talk? Please talk. Just say your name."

Rufus chimed in. "Yeah, Hannah. It's better when you talk. Then we can fix you up better. See? Look at me. I talked, and Mary made a new man out of me."

"Whatever you did, you did yourself, Ruf," I interrupted. "How about a game? Alphabet? Ghost?" I didn't want the boys to begin pushing Hannah, but Rufus was hard to sidetrack. Resentful of Hannah in the beginning, then indifferent, Rufus was now like the rest of us, unable to resist her as she began to grow. He persisted now.

"Listen, Hannah, I know you can talk. I just have this feeling. And if you talk and tell us what the matter is, then we'll fix it. See, I used to be scared all the time, but not any more, and it'll be the same for you. See—your biggest problem is not talking—and if you talk, that'll fix the problem." Rufus smiled, pleased with his logic, but Hannah put her hands over her ears.

To distract Rufus I said, "Hey, Ruf, what did the big firecracker say to the little firecracker?"

"Don't know," said Rufus. "What?"

"My pop's bigger than yours."

And now Hannah's smiling. Good. We're going to be all right. I sang again.

> "She'll be drivin' six white horses
>   when she comes (*clippety-clop*),
> She'll be drivin' six white horses
>   when she comes (*clippety-clop*) . . ."

We arrived at the tollbooth of Beardsley State Park. Thunder Mountain was only our nickname. Brian handed the toll keeper our two dollars and he waved us through. "Nice day to get out of the house with the kids."

I waved and called back, "Beats scrubbing floors." The kids dissolved in laughter. They loved having us mistaken for a family.

We drove past the old wooden lodge and

empty parking lot, down to the lake. During the summer it was possible to rent rowboats and canoes, but now the place was deserted, except for two green boats bobbing beside the dock.

As soon as I parked the car, the boys were out, running for the dock. We had been here several times in May and June of the year before, and they headed now for one of their favorite spots: out onto the dock and then flat on their stomachs, their faces pressed against the boards, their eyes peering down into the shadowy water world below, searching for fish. All children are intrigued by animals, but for my children, whose coordination was often awkward and difficult, the easy, effortless movements of fish were all-absorbing.

I walked toward the dock, stopping halfway between the boys and Hannah. She was still in the car, but she had the door open, her seat belt unfastened, and her feet over the edge. She was on the verge of getting out, so I walked onto the dock to give her a little more room.

The boys were calling to each other, their voices hollow echoes in the empty space beneath the dock.

"Look at that fish. Boy, is he big." That was Rufus.

"He big," echoed Jamie.

"No. That's no fish. A rock, that is a rock," proclaimed accurate Brian.

"It is too a fish. Hey, Mary, look—isn't that too a fish?"

I laughed at Rufus. "You figure it out. You've

got better eyes than I have." I had learned not to get trapped into taking sides in a minor argument.

Hannah was out of the car and all the way down to the beginning of the dock. She put one foot tentatively on the wooden boards, then slowly, carefully, the other. Just then Rufus jumped up and the dock swayed under his sudden shift of weight. Startled, Hannah retreated quickly to solid ground.

It must seem strange and precarious to her—a narrow wooden floor built out over water. I turned my back to where Hannah stood on the shore and pumped up and down a couple of times. The boys turned, surprised but not alarmed.

"Hey, Mary. What're you doing?"

I raced out toward them, then jumped and landed hard in a squat beside them. If this old dock could stand my running and jumping, Hannah would know that it could stand her cautious weight.

I reached for Jamie and tumbled over on my back, taking him with me. "Not a bad way to go to school, eh?"

From flat on my back, I looked down over my sweatshirt and jeans, and there, framed between my sneakers, was Hannah. She was back out on the dock again. This time, though, she had decided on a safer approach. Not daring to walk yet—height making the journey more perilous—she was down on all fours, crawling toward us on hands and knees.

This was no easy task. She crawled inside the long dress, inching it along with her, stopping every few feet to look back over her shoulder to see how far she'd come. As she neared us, we instinctively rearranged ourselves to make room for her. Finally, she arrived and lay down between us, panting, her face sweaty from exertion. But within a minute or two she had her eyes open and was looking through a crack down to the water below. The boys immediately began pointing out things to her.

"See that log, Hannah? That's where big fish, really big fish, live."

"Over there by the side, where those stones are, there was a penny there last summer."

"Look, Hannah, there, look at the fish—"

"That's not a fish. Doesn't move. It's a rock."

Suddenly I felt, more than saw, Hannah turn her face toward me. I turned my own head. One side of my face was pressed against the warm wooden boards, and while the fish swam silently beneath us, Hannah and I looked at each other. We were only inches apart, our noses almost touching. I could feel her breath, puffy and warm on my face. We stayed like this for perhaps one full minute. Hannah's eyes were wide open, the whites clear, almost translucent. The irises were layers of blue, lighter on the surface, then soft deep blue underneath. Bright sunlight framed Hannah's face as if in a close-up, and once again I was startled by the beauty and intelligence that were there.

Gone were the dumpy body and awkward clothes; her matted hair was only a blurred outline; her skin shone from exercise and the pleasure of success. All the things Hannah could be were clearly visible, and I silently promised her, I'll help, Hannah, trust me. Let's try again, okay?

We could have moved away from each other. It would have been easy for either of us to turn our head, but we stayed, silently looking at each other, until Hannah moved her arm—accidentally, purposely? It was impossible to tell, but she moved her arm until it lay against my own.

Finally the boys tired of watching the fish and ran off to turn over rocks along the water's edge, searching for snails, the possibility of finding a bloodsucker heightening their excitement.

I got up slowly and stretched out my hand to Hannah. She took it and we took a few slow steps back toward the shore. Then I stopped and rearranged her dress, pulling more of it over the string at her waist so that her legs were free and she could walk more easily. Soon I'd have to do something about her clothes and her hair. So much to do, but for now it was enough just to feel the sun, walk, be alive.

When we got to the end of the dock, we walked down and stood beside the boys on the shore. Hannah watched, and then we followed as they left the water and headed up the mountain, climbing one of the gently sloping trails, walking single file beneath pine trees, birches, oaks. Rufus raced ahead, clambering over fallen logs, sometimes leaving the path to climb a nearby boulder and shout down to us, exulting in his freedom. Brian walked slowly, trying to stay near Hannah while he gathered the golden leaves that had fallen from the oaks. Jamie and I brought up the rear. For these children who rarely left their homes and had never seen a snake or a frog, much less a porcupine needle, each step was an adventure.

At lunchtime we turned and went back to the lake, this time choosing the white sandy beach that bordered the east end, rather than the boat cove. We carried the food and a blanket from the car and spread the blanket on the sand. We ate there with the sand creeping over the edges of the blanket, mixing with the sandwiches, while the lemonade grew warm in the paper cups. It was all just right—a real picnic.

After lunch we dug hollows in the warm sun and dozed and told stories. Our stories were always make-believe, but make-believe that could be true. There was no one storyteller; we passed the stories around. One person began, another did the middle, and another the end.

"Once there was a cat with the longest tail in the world. It was so long that when he sat down he could wrap his tail around him three times. It was a beautiful tail, but the cat didn't like it because all the other cats ..."

Here someone would take over the story and continue until he ran out of ideas or wanted to see what someone else would say. We liked it because this kind of storytelling gave us another way to talk. Some of the things that were too big or too scary for regular talk could come out in a story.

After a while, we grew quiet again. Rufus picked up a book and wandered off to read. Jamie began building a castle, or maybe it was a mountain, and Hannah took off her shoes and socks and began to scrunch her toes back and forth in the sand. Then, evidently liking the feel of the sand, she got up and began to walk around us barefoot, in ever-increasing circles.

Brian stayed still beside me, turning a small stone over and over in his hand. I sat cross-legged, tracing letters in the damp sand, trying to listen to what Brian hadn't found words for yet. He got another stick, and after carefully patting the sand flat he drew people inside television sets. People safe in boxes—far away, not close or real. People were what troubled Brian. He could cope with letters, numbers, words, but people were difficult.

Finally he said, "What's school like? Real school, I mean."

Brian was obviously worrying about next year. He knew that this was his last year here. Twelve was the top age limit at the school.

"Well," I said, searching for words that would be reassuring and still honest, "it depends on what school you're talking about. I can tell you about the school where I went." I told him about the classrooms and the gym, the plays we put on, and our newspaper.

The newspaper interested him. "You had your own newspaper? How did you make it?"

I told him that in my first school we typed up stories and carved a woodcut for the masthead. By high school we had sports reporters and news reporters; we pasted up galleys, picked type for headlines, and finally had the pages printed by a professional printer.

"If I go," he asked. "I mean when I go to school, will they have a paper there?"

"I don't know," I said, "but if they don't, maybe you can start one. Just a little one at first, but I bet you could get one going."

He was quiet, but he seemed satisfied. "Maybe," he said, "maybe that new school won't be so bad." He paused and looked out toward the lake and then pointed. "Look at Hannah. Look at her there. Hannah's ... I think she's ... Mary, it looks like Hannah's dancing."

Brian was right. It did look like Hannah was dancing. She was down by the very edge of the lake, just where the water touched the sand, holding up her skirt in her hands, running along the water's edge. But though the sun was warm, the water was October cold, and when she went too close and water accidentally touched her bare feet, she hopped backwards or sideways to escape. Despite her heavy body, Hannah had a natural grace, and what might have seemed like awkward retreats in another child blended together in a smooth, natural rhythm. I loved to watch her. Inside Hannah, deep down beneath the rage, hurt, and humiliation, there was an indestructible center of joy. She had a true and natural joyful self.

The phrase stirred a memory, and I suddenly recalled a day when I was in the hospital for the birth of my second child. A friend brought me a bottle of wine and held it up before me. "For a joyful woman," she said. "This is how I always think of you." I don't know if it's true, but I love the quality of joy in other people. It's one thing that draws me to children. When a child is well and adequately nourished with food and love, almost always the joy tumbles out.

But for Hannah to have kept this through the terrors of her life—the operation, the beatings, the rejection and neglect—showed a quality of joy and strength that was awesome. Hannah had a strong sense of self. She knew who she was. As I watched I again questioned the psychologist's diagnosis. Autistic children have no awareness of who they are. I couldn't believe that Hannah was retarded or psychotic.

A cloud passed across the sun and I looked at my watch. Almost two o'clock. We had to hurry now to get back by two thirty, the offical ending of our day. Where had the hours gone? I wanted more. It was too soon to go back. I needed more time, but then this was true almost every day.

I rounded up the children and then packed the lunch things. I dried Hannah's feet with paper napkins and got her shoes and socks on and then urged everyone toward the car. The two-thirty deadline was no joke. Buses arrived, and these buses picked up other children at other schools. All sorts of schedules were thrown off and panic buttons pushed if the children weren't back on time.

But once in the car, everyone relaxed and all was well. The children, warm and sleepy from their day in the sun and fresh air, dozed or day-dreamed. I drove, happy and content at having them all there with me in the car.

After a little while, Rufus roused. He began humming a little and singing to himself. At first it meant nothing, but then I recognized a currently popular commercial.

"Oh, I wish I were an Oscar Meyer
    Weiner,
  That is what I'd truly love to be.
    'Cause if I were an Oscar Meyer Wiener,
  Then everybody'd be in love with me."

Brian opened his eyes and sang with Rufus the second time. The song was an instant success, and the boys got wider and wider awake. Jamie shouted out "me" and something close to "wiener" in almost the right places, and even Hannah turned her head.

Rufus was in seventh heaven. Everyone's attention was focused on him and he wasn't about to lose it. He lowered his voice to a conspiratorial whisper. "Want to hear the dirty version?"

If they were attentive before, they were riveted now. Rufus sang:

"Oh, I wish I were an Oscar Meyer
    Wiener,
That is what I'd truly love to be.
    'Cause if I were an Oscar Meyer Wiener,
Then everybody'd *pee* all over me."

The boys exploded in laughter and Hannah giggled. This version was even more successful than the first, and the children sang it over and over with delight.

I was silent driving down the highway, watching the boys in the rearview mirror, glancing sideways at Hannah. What was happening? I didn't know, couldn't put my finger on it, but some kind of excitement was building in the car. Something, something was about to happen.

When it did I almost didn't recognize it. At first I didn't even hear it. Not till Brian said, "Shhh," and Hannah said—*Hannah* said—"I sing song."

I wanted to pull off the highway, get out, stop traffic. But I knew I couldn't break the spell.

Hannah's voice was small and quiet, but it was clear and it filled the car.

"Oh, I wish I were a General Motors seat
    belt,
That is what I'd truly love to be,

'Cause if I were a General Motors seat
   belt,
Then everybody'd *shit* all over me!"

The boys and I sat in absolute silence. Where
had these full-blown, coherent sentences come
from? For two months in our classroom Hannah
had uttered nothing but grunts and groans and
howls. At home she evidently used a few words,
but not in school. If Hannah had said "Good" or
"Sing" we would all have been jubilant and vocif-
erous with our praise. But to have this, this whole
weird song, all at once was too much and we sat
in shocked silence, until suddenly Brian came to
and said, "Hannah. Sing it again. Please sing it
again."

Brian began the song himself and Rufus's voice
joined him and then Hannah's voice began again
and blended with theirs. This spontaneous approval was just what she needed. You never know,
I thought. You never know what shape a miracle
will have.

This was hardly approved teaching material.
But what did it matter? What did I care? Hannah
was singing. She had broken through her barricade of silence, and as they finished the second
round I joined the cheers.

"Sing it again, lovey," I said. "Go ahead and
sing it again."

Now that Hannah had spoken, it was important
to keep her language flowing. She had, of course,

done much more than utter an isolated word. She had used a complete sentence. "I sing song." She had taken Rufus's jingle and adapted it to express an idea of her own, a crude one, but that was not the point. What interested me was her ability to use expressive language.

I had known she had receptive language, that she could hear, perceive, understand what was spoken to her. Now she showed that she could use words to express an idea, if she wished.

With Hannah it was not going to be so much to teach her new words, although I was sure her vocabulary was limited. The crucial thing would be to create a climate in which she would want to talk. Obviously there were all kinds of words in her head. She even had a sense of syntax: "I sing song"—subject, followed by verb, followed by object. But she must have had these abilities before and just not used them.

In our school, a language difficulty was not unique. Over two thirds of our children had grave problems with verbal communication; it was one of the things that set them apart from other children. The world takes speech so for granted that people are shocked, even frightened, by a child without words.

In our own classroom, Jamie, Brian, and Hannah had each had severe language problems when they came. Rufus was different. He had used bizarre language when he was frightened, sitting behind his briefcase chanting weird nursery rhymes. "Little Jack Horner sat in a corner. He put in a thumb and pulled out—a tooth. Shouldn't eat pie. Should brush your teeth or you'll get cavities and your teeth will fall out." This wasn't a language problem. In fact, language helped because it gave Rufus a way to get some of his fears from the inside to the outside. But the other three all had real language problems. Jamie had had no words at all. He had less than a hundred now, and he had struggled hard to learn to say each one. But at least he knew his name, his address, his phone number and could say and write them all. If he should run again, if anger or fear exploded inside him and he ran, at least he could get back home.

Brian had been an elective mute, capable of speech but refusing to speak or, rather, refusing to speak coherently. Rather than trust us with his words, he had taught himself to speak in a weird jumble, like a speeded-up phonograph record. As he became more sure of himself, Brian was able to give up this cover of garbled speech and talk to us in normal sentences.

All three boys were growing—dealing with their problems, gradually overcoming them. Now Hannah. Could we keep Hannah talking to us?

The day after our picnic Hannah sat beside me at Best and Worst and Rufus said, before all our feet were even under the table, "Well—the best thing is easy. The best thing that happened since last time was the picnic. I sure do like those old

picnics. I could go on a picnic every day, every
single day, maybe even twice a day."

We all sat looking at him, remembering. I
waited a minute to see if anybody would ask a
question, but the children were silent, so I said,
"What part did you like best, Ruf? Was there one
special part of the picnic that you liked better than
the rest?"

"Sure. I always like the fish the best. Someday
I'm gonna go up there and catch one of those fish.
Boy, would my father ever be surprised if I
brought home a big old fish."

Brian said, "Not me. I liked—"

Rufus stood up. "It's not your turn. I didn't
even do the worst thing yet."

Brian ducked his head, rebuked, too easily hurt.
I had one arm around the back of Hannah's chair
in case she should decide to bolt. With my free
hand I touched Brian's arm. "It's your turn next,
Bri. Okay, Rufus. Go ahead. Do the worst thing."

Rufus picked up the father from the box in the
center of the table that held the doll family. "The
worst thing was my father yelling last night. I
hate it when he yells."

"Me too," Brian agreed, revitalized. "I hate it
when they yell."

"He yelled and then my mother yelled back.
She said he thought he knew everything. Is that
right, do you think? Does he know everything?"

"Does it seem like he does?" I asked.

Rufus thought. "Not everything. Sometimes he
just acts like he knows. Sometimes it's like

he's scared we'll find out he doesn't know everything."

I leaned toward Rufus. "You think it'd be scary—?"

"Time's up, Mary." Brian pointed to the clock. "He's had his five minutes. It's my turn. Right?"

There was never enough time. There were so many thoughts to follow. It was important to know all about each child, everything, the details as well as the main currents. But it was true that everybody had to have a turn. Circle lasted from nine thirty to ten, by the time the kids got back from the bathroom it was well after ten, and now it was already past ten twenty. There were still three more children to go—and we hadn't even begun reading or math.

"You're right. It's your turn, Bri. But Rufus, remember, and maybe we can talk after lunch." Reluctantly, Rufus relinquished the father doll to Brian.

"Put them all back," Brian said. "Have to put all the dolls back in the box when your turn's up." He carefully arranged the dolls so that the boy doll was close beside the mother. "The worst thing," he said, "was that the mother didn't come in to watch TV with me. Had to watch all alone."

Brian had a large color TV at the foot of his bed; most nights his mother watched television with him after dinner, preferring the color TV set to the small black and white set in the living

room. Many nights she dozed off as she watched—
and slept there until morning.

I had spoken to both Brian and his parents
about this situation and now I said again, "I
thought you were going to move the big TV out
to the living room, Brian. We talked about that
before, remember?"

Brian shook his head. "Can't. Can't move it.
Mimmie, Grandma Mimmie, is sleeping in the
dining room now. Daddy says the big set is too
noisy. It will keep Mimmie awake."

"It isn't any noisier than the little one. Anyway,
never mind." I would have to talk to the family
again, make them understand that Brian couldn't
continue to sleep with his mother. If only our psychiatrist had time to come to some of our parent-
teacher conferences. . . . "Your mom didn't watch
with you last night?"

"No. Wouldn't watch. Went to a Bingo game
with Mimmie and then went to bed in Daddy's
room."

Three cheers for Bingo.

"Hey, Brian, hurry up. You only got one minute
left, you know. You can't have extra time. You
wouldn't let me. You didn't even do the best thing
yet," said Rufus.

"I know," Brian said. He said it so softly that
we all turned to look at him. Forget the TV in his
bedroom—listen to him now. Listen to the best
thing. "I know," he repeated. "I know the best
thing. The picnic."

"That's not fair!" shouted Rufus. "That's my best thing. That's not fair, Mary, is it?"

"Hush, Ruf. Let him finish. It's his turn."

"The picnic," Brian said again. Then he picked up the girl doll and turned directly toward Hannah. "The girl, Hannah, talked at the picnic. That was the best."

If there are natural lovers anywhere, they must be children. Even with all his troubles, Brian thought about Hannah. For him, the best thing of the day was that she talked.

I reached across the table and hugged him. "Yes, she did. Hannah talked, and it sure was a best thing."

Brian put the girl doll back in the doll family box on the table. Immediately Hannah reached for it, standing the doll firmly, squarely, on her feet. Then with her eyes on Brian she declared strongly, staunchly, "I not talk good picnic. I sing song. I talk now."

All three boys stared at Hannah. Brian's eyes never left her face.

Hannah stood up, still holding the girl doll. "Now I talk good. Say hello. Hello Jay-me, hello Roofs, hello Bri-an."

We all looked at Hannah without speaking, almost as though we were afraid to break the spell.

Then Rufus said, "Hey, Hannah. You forgot Mary. Say hello to her too. Say, 'Hello, Mary.' "

But Hannah shook her head and my heart sank. Would I be refused? Would she speak to the others but not to me? Had past schools made too many mistakes? Had I, too, already hurt her so much that she wouldn't speak to me? I lowered my eyes. What could I do?

Before I could think I felt a hand on my shoulder and I looked up to find Hannah's eyes only inches from mine.

"Hello," she said. "Hello, teacher."

9

Almost every day for the next six weeks, Hannah set a new milestone. There was no stopping her now. She was not just learning; she was insisting that I teach her all that I could—and she made this clear. The boys always called me Mary, but Hannah addressed me as "teacher" as though to remind us both.

I called all the children by their first names and an affectionate nickname or two. I called Hannah "Hannah" or sometimes "babe" or "lovey" as I had my own daughter when she was small. The terms of affection slipped out easily, naturally, so easily that I was hardly aware of using them.

But Hannah was aware. She came to me one noontime as I sat on the little stoop outside our door, searching out whatever sunlight I could find while I watched the children play. The November sunshine was thin and cool, but still some inner part of me was warmed by it. Perhaps it was energy, not heat, that I sought. Who knows? Maybe we have some kind of inner solar collector that stores energy from the sun.

A shadow crossed my face and I looked up to

see Hannah peering down at me. "You getting suntan, teacher?"

"Hey, Hannah, hello. You surprised me. There's not much sun. What can I do for you?" I asked.

She stood unsmiling. "Not Hannah. Not call Hannah. Call me lovey. I like that lovey. Nobody said that before."

I pulled her down into my lap. "Okay, now. Lovey, lovey, lovey, lovey. Hullo there, Hannah lovey."

Hannah's head lay in my lap, her eyes almost smiling. I brushed her hair back from her forehead and hit a cold hard wad of gum.

"Listen," I said. "It's time to get this mess of gum out of your hair. How did you get it in there anyway?"

Hannah pushed my hand away, shook her head, and hunched her shoulders down into my lap. It was obvious that she didn't want to talk about it, but we were going to have to get the gum out sooner or later, and I decided to pursue it a little further now.

"Let's get some scissors and cut it out. I'll be careful and go slowly and it won't hurt, I promise."

Hannah sat up. "No," she said. Clearly, definitely. "No cut hair." Hannah wasn't going to give in easily.

"Okay," I said. "No big thing. We can wait if you like those lumps of gum so much. A regular walking gum machine, you are."

The smile was out of Hannah's eyes now.

"Mine," she said, putting her hand over her hair. "Mine."

"Okay. You're right. It's your hair. I won't cut the gum out until you want me to."

But I had underestimated Hannah's courage. The next morning she arrived at school looking like a victim of brain surgery. Great bald patches showed through the remaining long, dirty hair, and there were dark bruises from little sleep beneath her eyes. The lumps of gum were gone, but so was most of her hair.

She went straight to the coat closet and sat down. I followed and sat beside her in the dim warmth and held her face between my hands. "It's okay, lovey. It'll grow. You were good to cut the gum out."

She looked straight at me. "Mine. Mine hair. Me cut."

"I see you did. I understand you wanted to do it yourself. You wanted to cut your own hair."

"Fix," she commanded. "Fix hair now, teacher."

Impatience and sorrow mingled in her voice as her fingers explored the barren, stubby areas where she had chopped her hair away.

I looked down at the disaster of Hannah's head. What could be done? How did she think that I could make it right? Did she believe I could somehow transplant hair?

"It'll be all right, babe," I said again. "It'll grow. Hair grows fast."

This wasn't good enough for Hannah. She shook her head and pulled me toward the art

cabinet, tugged open the door, and handed me a
child's pair of scissors.

"Fix," she pleaded.

"You want me to cut it? Is that it? You want me
to make it even?"

She stood still, not understanding, not knowing
the word "even," but trusting, waiting patiently.
In three months she had come a long way. I
couldn't let her down now.

Perhaps I could take her to my own hair-
dresser—to Vincent—who cut my hair with easy
expertise each month. But then, remembering the
white coats, the rows of hair driers and curious
women, I discarded the idea.

"Okay," I said. "But if I'm going to do it, I'm
going to do it right. Brian, will you go down to
the office and get Zoe's big scissors?"

Brian scampered out the door.

"Now, we need a mirror and a comb."

I got the large table mirror that I had bought
years before to use for speech. I arranged it on
the desk with my comb and draped an old sheet
from the paint cupboard under the chair.

Hannah sat down, staring at herself in the mirror. Involuntarily her hand moved up—touching
her hair, her face. She turned to look at me, then
back to the mirror, leaning forward to touch her
reflection.

"Mine?" she asked.

Suddenly I knew that she had never used a
mirror before, that this was the first time she had
ever looked at herself. Quickly I knelt down

beside her so that my face was reflected in the mirror beside hers. This teaching is like Pandora's box—once opened, each small thing leads to still another.

"Yes," I said, touching her face. "That's you." And then, touching mine, "This is me."

Hannah touched my face, watching all the while in the mirror.

"You," she said. "Me." Then, patting the mirror, "It make picture you and me, teacher."

"Yes, it's a mirror and it shows, makes a picture, of whoever's in front of it. See, here's Jamie, here's Rufus," I said, nudging the boys into view. "The picture doesn't last, though. It's only there when we are."

Hannah nodded. Then she went back to studying herself in the mirror, touching eyes, nose, and mouth. I must get a bigger mirror so that she can see all of herself, I thought, so that they can all see and get to know and understand their bodies. I should have done this before.

"Tomorrow," I promised, "I'll bring a big mirror, a long one so you can see all of yourself at once."

Brian arrived with the scissors and Hannah settled into the chair. The three boys lined up behind me.

"You gonna give Hannah a haircut, Mary?" asked Rufus.

"Mm-hmm."

"Where'd you learn how to do that?"

"Oh, it's easy," I said. "Nothing to it."

But Rufus was right. I hadn't ever cut anyone's hair before. Snip. I held a long limp strand in my left hand and cut it with the scissors. The boys gasped as Hannah's hair fell on the sheet, and I stopped, feeling as though I had severed some live, vital part of her.

"Fix. Not so slow. Fix," Hannah commanded, utterly sure that I could do it.

"Okay. I'm fixing. You can't rush a good hair-cut."

There was obviously no way out, so I snipped and cut, trying to remember how Vincent layered my hair, trying to angle sections of hair so they would fall over the bald spots.

By the time I finished, I felt as though I had run twenty miles uphill and I could hear Brian let out a long sigh of relief, but there reflected in the mirror was Hannah's round little face framed with soft uneven hair.

I gave the scissors to Brian to return and took Hannah to the bathroom and washed her hair with clear, warm water and then rubbed it almost dry with a towel. Now that Hannah's hair was shorter and a little cleaner, it curved around her cheeks and the red-gold color was more pronounced.

Back in the classroom I put away the mirror and the sheet and then went to the furnace room to get a broom and dustpan to sweep up the long strands of hair still on the floor. I stopped in a corner of the furnace room and sighed. Weariness mingled with frustration. Another hour gone, another day almost over, and math still not done. The science experiment I had planned not even begun. Tomorrow, tomorrow, I promised myself. Nothing will interrupt. Tomorrow we'll get caught up on academics. How did this happen? How did I get into these things, anyway?

As I came back into our room carrying the broom and dustpan, I realized that the outside door was open and Hannah wasn't inside. What now? Where had she gone?

This was too much. Irritation laced my voice. "Where's Hannah?" I said to the boys. "Where'd she go?"

They looked silently back at me and Brian pointed to the door.

"Obviously," I said. "I can see that she went out the door, but where is . . ."

As I was talking, I walked over to the door. It was immediately evident why the boys were unable to find words.

There on the stoop where I had sat the day before was Hannah. She had dragged out two small chairs, arranged them so they faced each other, and had stretched out on them, her cropped head tipped back, her eyes closed, her face turned toward the pale November sun.

"Hannah. What are you doing?" I asked, although I already knew. I could feel a warm fullness rising in my throat. I struggled to keep irritation in my voice, but it had already melted somewhere and I said only, "Come back in now, lovey. Your hair's still damp and you'll catch cold."

Hannah turned her head and smiled at me, her face radiant beneath the sunlit halo of her hair. "In minute. I getting suntan, teacher. Like you."

10

Hannah's days were always full. She'd never had a chance to do all the small, ordinary things that children do at home or in kindergarten. Her anger and disruptive behavior had made it impossible for her to explore and learn. But now she colored and drew pictures on whatever paper I could find: newsprint, waxed paper, aluminum foil, even sandpaper. She liked the different feel and look of each piece, and her fingers grew more and more deft as she colored and painted. She used chalk and paints and crayons, and sometimes all three at once.

Occasionally I took one of her paintings home and ran it through my sewing machine. Without thread, the needle perforated the paper, and in school the next day Hannah cut carefully along the lines to make her own picture puzzle. New discoveries like this always delighted her, and her high, sweet voice would sing out over our classroom. "Oh, boy, teacher. See. See picture."

Brian and Rufus would stop and smile almost as often as I did. We were all caught up in her pleasure and excitement in learning.

Hannah came with us to Circle now. She didn't

talk there; she just sat beside me, one hand in my lap, watching everything that happened. But one day Patty brought in some of her records and we saw a new side of Hannah. She danced all over the room—she did the Twist, the Wiggle, and a dozen different dances I didn't know the names of. But Hannah knew what she was doing, and she did it with style and grace and an odd touch of sophistication.

Back in our classroom, she was a child again. We had all kinds of letters and numbers stored in painted or covered coffee cans; sandpaper letters, wooden letters from old anagram games, magnetic letters—even alphabet macaroni. Hannah loved them, and she sorted and matched them hour after hour.

Sometimes we played homemade games of Lotto or Bingo. At first she just matched the wooden letter to a letter on the board. Later she learned names and I would say the name of a letter, holding it in my hand without letting her see it, and she would find it on the board.

She played dominoes, matching the dots. She lined cans and sticks up according to size. She learned the meaning of above and below, same and different. She learned to classify objects by color, use, and other qualities. She loved drawing pictures of herself. I brought in a long roll of brown paper, and Hannah and Jamie each lay down flat on it while I traced around them. Brian and Rufus were too old for this sort of thing, but they helped the other two cut the figures out and paint them with bright colors.

One day I set up the easel with a large sheet of lined story paper and put two small chairs in front of it, one for Hannah and one for me. "Okay," I said. "Today we're going to write a story. We'll do it together, but it will really be your story. I'll just write it down here for you." I pointed to the large story paper and waggled my Magic Marker.

Hannah came and sat beside me and stared at the blank paper.

"There are lots of things we can write about," I said. "I'll make a list of three things here that I think of and then I'll make a list of three things you think of—and then we'll choose one of them."

Hannah looked at me sadly. "Can't think. Can't think no story."

"It's not your turn yet. Just wait a minute, okay? It's my turn now. Let's see. . . . We could write about food—hot food, cold food, breakfast, lunch—"

"Dessert," Hannah interrupted. "Not write food. Write dessert."

Carefully I wrote *Food*. "This is my list," I said. "I want food. You can write dessert on yours if you want."

Hannah was out of her chair watching every letter that I wrote. I had her. I had her now. Hannah didn't know it yet, but today was to be her first reading lesson.

We had already spent hours during the last

week on what the books call "reading readiness." Hannah knew the letters of the alphabet. She could recognize them easily, call them by name, even write them. The sounds of the letters were much harder for her, particularly the vowels, and I knew that if Hannah was ever to learn to read it would have to be much more with her eyes than her ears. It was not until much later that I learned the terms visual and auditory dyslexia, but I did know that Hannah had to have early success and that this was much more possible for her visually than any other way.

"So I'll have food and—ah, books and houses for my three." As long as I had caught her interest with food, I tried to make the other subjects more vague and less interesting.

"Dessert," Hannah said. "I like dessert."

"Okay, that's a pretty good opening sentence. Let's store our other ideas for now and do this one."

I turned to a new piece of paper and across the top I printed DESSERT.

"That's our title, Dessert."

Beneath it I printed, "I like dessert," reading it out loud as I wrote.

Hannah was standing close beside me, her cropped hair almost touching the paper.

"What kind of dessert do you like?" I asked.

"Cake. I like cake."

Carefully I printed the next line, saying it. "I like cake."

"And I like pie too," Hannah said.

This child—why had it taken so many years? She was so easy to teach. I added, "I like pie," saying it, writing it, and almost before I was through Hannah said, "And I love ice cream."

"Okay. Good. That's a great clincher. That'll be our last line: 'And I love ice cream.'"

Our paper now read:

DESSERT

I like dessert.
I like cake.
I like pie.
And I love ice cream.

I put down the Magic Marker and said to Hannah, "I'm going to read this story of yours now, okay?"

She nodded and I put my hand under the title. "Dessert." My hand moved to the first line as I read slowly and with as much feeling as I could get into it, "I—like—cake," my hand underlining each word as I read it. When I reached the last line I read it with even more emotion. "And I *love* ice cream.

"Okay, now, Hannah. It's your turn. We'll start right here with the title." I took her hand and placed it under the word at the top of the paper.

"Dessert?" she asked, uncertainly, looking at me.

"Yes, sure. Now look here. See, this is the word, right? These are the letters that make the word 'dessert': D-E-S-S-E-R-T." I wasn't concerned with word-attack skills. All I wanted was for Hannah to get the idea that letters made up words and that every spoken word had its written counterpart. I drew her fingers along, beneath the letters.

"Dessert," she said.

"Yes, indeed." I moved her hand to the next line and placed it under the first word.

"I. I know letter, that I ... E-F-G-H-I."

"Yes. You're right. It's the letter 'I' and it's the word 'I.' Now look here. What did you say you like?"

"I like cake." I moved Hannah's hand beneath the words as she said them.

"Great. Good. Now the next line." I placed her hand below the third line of printing.

"I ... I like pie."

Excitement was catching in her voice as comprehension crept in. The words were her words. The words on the paper were the words she had spoken.

"And," she shouted, "I *love* ice cream!"

"Well, what do you know, hotshot. You read the whole story."

"Do it again, teacher. Read. You read."

Hannah was so excited now she couldn't stand still. She jumped up and down in little hops beside me as I read the page again, underlining each word as I said it.

"Me. I. Me. . . . No. I read story now."

Over and over Hannah read her story, each time more pleased, until finally I said, "We forgot something. You wrote the story. It's your story. The person who writes the story always signs it."

I handed Hannah the felt pen and slowly, carefully, she lettered "Hannah" on the bottom of the page. Then she turned to me.

"Hang up. Hang up story, teacher."

I taped Hannah's story to the front wall of our classroom, beside Jamie's pictures and Rufus and Brian's papers.

Now we had more of Hannah in our room than just her name beneath her coat hook. Her story hung on the wall with the others.

I used anything I could think of to keep Hannah going during this first white-hot excitement of learning. Best and Worst, the doll family—repetition of her words to show her that I heard what she was saying and that I considered it vitally important, important enough to write down. I wanted to give her all the feedback that I could, good accurate feedback to show her, without saying it, that she was good and was getting even better, as a yardstick with which to measure herself.

Hannah wrote story after story until finally there was no more space on the walls of our room. She loved each story better than the one before and walked the floor reading them out loud to herself.

We wrote them all in the same manner as we had the first one, and though the sentences grew a little longer and the words somewhat more varied, they were all essentially the same. They were all about things that were important to Hannah, like colored chalk, red and yellow marbles, our housekeeping corner, blocks, the doll family, her own family.

From the stories, she copied individual words onto index cards. She kept these cards in bundles, bound with rubber bands, inside her cubby. Every day she laid her cards out on the floor and practiced them. Later she brought them to me so that I could hear her say them.

This type of reading now has the formal name Language Experience. Whole volumes have been written about it and the "word banks" (Hannah's index cards in a recipe box) that accompany it and its effectiveness as a method of teaching reading.

It's a good way to learn to read. It's personal, exciting, and highly individualized and always has been. From the beginning of our written language men have been telling stories, writing them down, and then reading and rereading them.

There are only a couple of things to check to make sure this type of reading instruction works. First, the child should be a visual rather than an auditory learner and have good visual memory skills. Second, the word bank should be checked against the Dolch sight words (200 most common words) and then against graded vocabulary lists, which can be made up from the vocabulary in the back of any basal reading series. Most of the words that come naturally from a child's speech will be duplicated in these lists, but it's helpful to have the lists to make sure that the child is moving forward at a steadily increasing level of difficulty. And last—the only thing that is really important—it must be fun.

When there was no more room left on the walls, we began to make books. We wrote Hannah's stories on blank paper that I lined on one side, punched with holes across the top, and put between two shirt cardboards. I laced the pages together with yarn. Hannah drew with crayons on the cardboard cover and then drew on the blank side of the paper to make a picture for the story beneath it. Hannah's books pleased me almost as much as they did Hannah, and I took them to the Director and to staff meetings.

I rejoiced in Hannah's talking even more than in the reading or writing. Her speech was still limited and she stuttered slightly; in her eagerness, syntax remained unfathomable. But if grammatical expression was poor, style and content were superb.

Happiness bubbled and surfaced at Best and Worst and enchanted the boys as well as me.

"Best thing today Grandpa." Sparklers light inside Hannah's eyes and tiny firecrackers of laughter go off in her throat.

"What about Grandpa?"

"Grandpa live downstairs. Grandpa cross. Make everybody mind. Make everybody do thing *he*

want. Make Mama cook dinner every day five
o'clock. Make Mama shut windows, pull down
shades. Make Mama sit living room downstairs till
he go sleep. Make me stay kitchen. Boss Mama.
Boss Helen. Boss me. Boss Carl, too."

Hannah stops and shakes her head.

"But Little Caesar no mind him." Her laughter
begins again. She's so pleased with something, she
can't contain it.

"Who's Little Caesar?" Rufus wants to know.

"Little Caesar Grandpa's dog. Grandpa scare
Little Caesar, too. Last night Little Caesar fix
Grandpa."

Hannah looks us over, making sure she has our
full attention before she whips out the climax of
the story.

"Caesar bark go out. Grandpa yell, not let Caesar out, Caesar pee on Grandpa's light cord. Light
cord broken. Caesar pee. *Whoozz! Fuiei! Arf! Arf!*
All fireworks. No lights. Mama say Caesar he
short-circuit Grandpa."

What a story! The boys even let Hannah run
over her allotted five minutes, they were so enchanted with her tale.

After we had finished Best and Worst, Hannah
got a pencil and drew the story. The two-family
house, Grandpa's living room, the broken light
cord, and a short, wiry-looking dog with one leg
raised. Then we wrote it down, another story for
her book. It was my favorite, but all her stories
were vivid and complete.

If there was buoyancy and joy inside Hannah, there was also seething rage. At least three or four times a week Hannah's anger exploded in our classroom, leaving desolation in its wake.

It was impossible to determine the cause of Hannah's anger. There seemed to be no common factor to what set the fuse or to the magnitude of explosion. Sometimes it was as small a thing as a crayon that broke under too much pressure. Hannah would try to put it back together; when this failed, she would hurl it—and the remaining crayons—across the room. She grunted, tore at her hair, and eventually went down onto the floor on her hands and knees to alternately rock and bang her head against the floor.

Sometimes the anger was caused by more than a small frustration. Sometimes one of the other children, particularly one of Patty's girls, would steal her lunch, ridicule her, or tease her beyond endurance. Occasionally a volunteer aide from another classroom (we had yet to be assigned an aide, the Director commenting that we seemed to be doing fine without one) or a parent, or another teacher would ask her to do something beyond her capabilities. Immediately Hannah would burst, and the party or play would be destroyed.

It wasn't right and I knew it. It wasn't fair to the other children or to Hannah herself, but I didn't know how to control it.

Anger was no stranger to me. Fear and loneliness and anger were daily enemies. All the children came locked within walls built of these ingredients, and I'd learned to acknowledge and deal with my own emotions as well as the children's.

It was the extent of Hannah's anger that was so difficult—that and the self-destruction. When she began to pound her head against the hard tile floor, she did it with such intensity that it seemed as though she wanted to crack it open and rid herself of the demons that drove her.

I talked to the Director. I talked to the psychiatrist and the psychologist. Their answers were the same. "You seem to be on the right track, Mary. Hannah's doing so well. You can't expect things to happen too quickly."

But I wasn't on the right track and I knew it deep in my bones. I was doing it wrong, and I longed for someone to help us both.

When the anger struck I went to Hannah, wanting to be near her, to protect her against the ravages of her own rage. I held her from behind, pinioning her arms so that she was unable to throw chairs or attack me. As she slipped toward the floor I stayed with her, trying to soften the driving head blows. But nothing seemed to help. Although she was eating, talking and reading, anger ruled her and poisoned our classroom.

The boys retreated when Hannah's anger struck. They were frightened and upset. They hated it when their own families fought, and now to have this raging emotion in our classroom almost every day was too much.

After a weekend of almost solid walking (I walk when I need to think), I decided that Hannah was manipulating me. Just as she had been a tyrant in her home and in previous schools on almost every issue, so she was now using rage in our room and I was letting her get away with it.

There was a gut feeling of truth to this, but I needed more. What to do? Go back, think back to the beginning. How did I first meet Hannah? What was my approach? How did I decide to handle her?

The immediacy of our school is such that it's hard to find time to remember. Days are filled with the sounds of children and skyrockets of emotion and there is no time for the slow, cool pause of reflection.

Coolness. Tranquillity. . . . That was it. Reason. I needed to approach Hannah with reason. Her intelligence: that was my first idea for approach, deciding to reach Hannah through her intelligence.

And instead I had been caught up in emotion. She had trapped me in the heat and intensity of her feelings, and my emotions had been aiding and abetting her own.

Hannah had seduced me into joining her. My support, my attention, had heightened the outbursts rather than modulating them.

On Monday morning, after Best and Worst, I said, "There isn't going to be any more yelling, screaming, throwing, or whatever in this room. I will give one warning to whoever is doing whatever it is that I don't like, and then if he or she continues I'll take away a privilege."

We spent another hour making up the lists of privileges. Another project went undone. Never mind, forget the Thanksgiving favors we were going to make.

The list-making was a long, cool, logical process and it was just what we needed. First on the blackboard, then on chart paper, we listed three "privileges" for each child. Each list was different, and all four children helped compile each list. Hannah's was as follows:

HANNAH'S PRIVILEGES

1. Colored chalk
2. Housekeeping corner
3. Dessert

Simple things, but our lives were made up of simple things. These were all things that Hannah liked, but most of all she liked dessert. The new plan was to work like this: If Hannah threw a book, I was to say, "Hannah, pick it up. Get back to work. This is a warning."

All the children felt very strongly about having a warning. They readily accepted losing privileges for poor behavior, but only if there was one clear warning first.

If, say, Hannah continued to throw things, I

was to say, "No colored chalk today, Hannah. You've lost that privilege."

If she stopped, that was all. If she continued, she was then to lose the privilege of playing in the housekeeping corner, and if she still continued she would lose her favorite, her beloved dessert.

There were many weaknesses to the plan. But at least we had a course of action and we'd worked it out together. It was to go into effect immediately.

Five minutes after we got up from the discussion, Hannah grabbed first one record out of Jamie's hands and then another and lost the privilege of colored chalk. Two minutes later she lost the privilege of playing in the housekeeping corner. This subdued her, though, and she sat sullenly on the stoop as the boys and I played ball in the driveway before lunch.

The rest of the day was uneventful and it seemed we were on the right track. No longer was I drawn into Hannah's anger; no longer did I feed it, reward it. Instead, I dealt with it coolly, from across the room.

The rest of the week worked as well. Almost every day, or at least every other day, Hannah lost one or two privileges. Jamie once lost two, Rufus one, Brian none at all. Instead, Brian drew his telethon on the blackboard, where he restored as prizes all the privileges that were lost.

On Friday, Hannah worked well for the first hour and then stormed through the second. There went the colored chalk, followed by the house-

keeping corner. I had to concentrate to keep my
voice cool as she gouged her pencil into Jamie's
clay letters that had taken him half an hour to
make, and I said, "Okay, Hannah. You just blew
dessert."

At first she didn't believe I meant it, but when
everyone was served except her, she threw a tantrum on the floor beside the lunch table and then
another in the classroom after lunch. There was
still no dessert, however.

Little by little, it dawned on Hannah that I
meant what I said. There was no longer any way
to draw the rest of us into her passion, to control
and manipulate us with her rage. Now anger
made her the loser.

Day after day Hannah blew dessert, and finally
she wept. But softly. The storms of rage subsided
into small rivers of tears.

Hannah's mother arrived unexpectedly after
school one day, and I rose in surprise to greet her.
Although we had had several conferences and
many, many phone calls, she had never come in
unannounced, of her own volition, before.

Now she stood in the doorway, surveying the
empty classroom, looking at me as I walked
toward her. I wanted to show her Hannah's stories, pictures, books. But she clearly had no time
for anything but what was on her mind.

"What," she demanded, no longer hesitant, no
longer shy, "what is this blue dessert?"

"Well—" I began.

Mrs. Rosnic was obviously agitated and she interrupted. "What you doing? All afternoon, all night, she howl about blue dessert, blue dessert, till it drive us all crazy. I give her blueberry pie. I try grape soda. But she yell, 'No! No! Blue dessert. Blue dessert.' I tell you—whatever—give to her. Here. I pay for it. Whatever. Just give to her the blue dessert so she stop the noise and we got peace."

"Okay," I said. "Okay, come on in, Mrs. Rosnic. I'll show you what it is."

Her broad, kind face creased in puzzlement as I got Hannah's chart of privileges down from the wall.

"Come on in," I said. "Please. This blue dessert is going to take a while."

11

The first snow of the year fell at night, so softly, so quietly, that I didn't even know that it had snowed until I woke the next morning. By then the sun was out making fractured rainbow patterns of the icy surface and the world was wrapped in glitter white like a big Christmas present begging to be opened.

School was a mass of confusion. Buses were late or nonexistent. The phone rang constantly in the Director's office. Parents, children, bus drivers milled around as I pushed through searching for Henry, our janitor, gardener, and friend. I needed to find the mission boxes.

The ladies of the church brought their families' worn-out clothing for the "mission boxes," and here, with the help of Henry, I stole clothes for the children whenever I needed them.

During the winter while the flowers lay dormant under snow or frozen ground, Henry hibernated in a corner of the furnace room. He worked a little during the middle of the day, making small repairs around the church or polishing the wooden cabinets in the kitchen. But mornings and afternoons he spent reading or dozing, dry and warm in an old chair near the furnace.

Sometimes I took my morning coffee and sat with him, studying the pictures that he pointed out in his seed catalogs or telling him about the children. Now I called to him impatiently. "Hey, Henry, where did you put the mission boxes? I'm going to need some things."

The children had warm clothes of their own, but their parents often forgot boots or gloves or an extra sweater in the turmoil of getting ready for school. Besides, they had no way of knowing that I'd take the children outside in the snow.

Henry led me upstairs to rows of cartons stacked on the back of the stage behind dark velvet curtains. They were full to the brim and we sorted through them, picking out scarves, warm sweaters, mittens.

"One more hat and I'm all set, Henry. Oh, good!"

Henry held up a small red knit cap with a missing tassel. "Be good for the boy. The little fellow."

"Jamie. Yes. You've got a good eye, Henry. It should be just right. Thanks for helping me. Does it bother you, my taking these clothes from church boxes?"

Henry continued to poke in the boxes. "They say they're for the 'needy.' They never said which needy."

As he was talking I spotted a navy blue sailor

dress in one of the boxes. I nudged it a little, considering. Would it fit Hannah? Would it be a good idea to find her a dress? Would it matter if it was secondhand?

The dress had a square white collar and a red tie. There were gold stars in each corner of the collar. The stars made up my mind.

"Can I take the sailor dress, too?" I asked.

He lifted it out of the box. It was wrinkled, with a small tear on the sleeve, but the material itself was soft and clean. Henry smoothed it out with his rough, gnarled hands. Working with flowers is not so different from working with children. "For the girl," he said.

"Yes. I think it'll fit. I can mend it tonight."

I put the dress in a paper bag on the closet shelf of our room. I gave the caps and mittens and scarves to the children, and we were dressed and ready and off to the graveyard across the street before it was time for Circle. The cemetery was quiet and protected and made a perfect play yard for the children.

The snow was only a few inches deep, but it changed the world. Trees were intricate ice sculptures, glinting in the sun. The pebble paths and brown grass were gone. It was a monochromatic scene, white and hushed.

At first the children were cautious, walking carefully, looking at each separate footprint they made, silent in a silent world. But I didn't want them moving with such prudence. I bent and scooped up a loose handful of snow, packed it together lightly, and tossed it over the top of Brown's mausoleum, then another over the Johnson monument, one more above the Ewing tombstone.

The children watched in awe, but snow is meant for fun and within minutes they forgot to be careful and began making their own snowballs, tossing them in the air, bombarding each other, laughing, running, hiding behind tombstones, pushing, tumbling in the snow with each other.

I stood still watching them. There is nothing in the world like play. If children can learn to play, they can learn to do almost anything.

The skirt of Hannah's long dress got wet and soggy and dirty and I tied it up, remembering with pleasure the sailor dress on the top shelf of the closet.

My sewing skills are primitive, but that night I found some navy blue thread and darned the tear, opened the seams and let out about two inches, and then rinsed out the dress and blocked it on a towel in the bathroom. In the morning before I left for school, I pressed the dress and folded it in tissue paper and put it back inside the paper bag.

I waited all morning looking for the right moment, but it never came. Finally, after lunch, the boys asked if they could ride their bikes in the driveway where the snow had already melted and disappeared.

Hannah had never learned to ride a bike. When she tried, her long dress tangled in the wheel chains, making it impossible. So now she stayed inside with me.

I left the outside door open so I could hear the boys, but my eyes were on Hannah as I lifted down the paper bag and laid the dress out on a table. "This is for you," I said to her. "A dress that's shorter, so that it will be easier for you to run and you can learn to ride without getting all tangled up."

Hannah came and touched the dress, not lifting it from the table, just poking it here and there. Then, looking at me for permission, she picked it up and took it into the closet, where she inspected all new things. After a few minutes, she came back and put the dress in my hands. "No good," she said gravely. "I too big. Too fat."

"Maybe," I said. "But I don't think so. Here, let's try."

I moved as gently, as slowly as I could, knowing how difficult it would be for her to take off the long housedress in which she even slept. It must by now be like a second skin. Without it she would be uncovered, bare and vulnerable.

Hannah stood absolutely still as I unbuttoned her dress until it was entirely open and then eased it off her shoulders, over one arm, over the other. She was naked now except for cotton underpants that hung on her hips below her bulging middle. A scar, three inches long, ran across her stomach.

Suddenly Hannah began to talk, words tumbling out faster than ever before. She pointed to the scar. "See. That from operation. That what make me funny. Had operation when I baby. They give me too much sleep stuff. Sleep stuff make me retard. Carl say that why I have to go to retard school."

Tears stood in her eyes, but she continued.

"Carl say that every morning, but Mama say no. She say I lucky be alive." Hannah gave a long sigh, nodding her head as though to convince us both. "Better than dead."

I gathered her up, forgetting to be careful, caring only about her fears and the draft from the outside door.

"Listen, lovey," I said. "You're no retard. Carl's the one that's dumb if he can't see that. Look how you're reading, making your own books. You've always been smart, never dumb. You just haven't been bothering to learn. Come on now, try your dress on."

She put it over her head and I pulled it down over her middle. (It did stick a little and I was glad I'd let out the seams.)

"Ah," I said. "You're beautiful. You are absolutely beautiful. Come see."

I led her to the long mirror I'd brought from home and watched as she smoothed the soft wool down across her front. Her exposed legs were round and pretty. Her blue eyes seemed even bluer. "Nice," she said. "It really nice, teacher."

"All right, now. Let's go show off. Let's show the Director and the boys."

But Hannah had her own ideas. "Now go bike riding."

I got our heavy jackets from the closet and then we went down to the Director's office, which among other things served as a garage for our donated bikes during the winter.

"Look at you, Hannah! A regular fashion plate," the Director said, and, to me, "Where'd it come from?"

I pointed upward, meaning the church.

The Director assumed more, or pretended she did, and raised her eyebrows. ". . . in mysterious ways His wonders to perform. . . ."

Hannah tugged impatiently at my arm. "Bike. Teach bike riding now."

"Ah, you. Okay. Here we go," and I began to disentangle a small two-wheeler equipped with training wheels.

"No," Hannah said. "Not that. That baby bike." She pointed to the full-sized red bike I usually rode. "That one. I ride that one. I big. I smart. You say I smart. I not ride retard bike."

I helped her on and then ran beside the bike holding onto the handlebars while she pedaled, pedaled with her lovely, beautiful, free bare legs.

Henry and Zoe and the Director came and stood in the driveway and cheered as we passed them, and the boys, hearing the noise, circled back to us shouting, "Hey, Hannah! Look at Hannah!"

Within another week Hannah was riding by herself, and the boys formed a vanguard for her as she rode up and down the driveway.

12

The Board of Directors of the school gave a cocktail party for the staff the second Saturday of December. I was less than eager to go, but when I told the Director that I thought I'd skip it, she frowned slightly and said, "It's important that you go, Mary."

This same Board of Directors had spearheaded the fund drive for the new school. They had done a magnificent job rounding up wealthy friends and getting in touch with influential people in foundations and had contributed generously themselves. The money was in now, the architect's drawings complete; ground would be broken in another few months. The Director's dream, a school of her own, was close to reality. No more borrowed church buildings or ancient houses. She would have a new building designed to her specifications, complete with kitchen and swimming pool, built particularly for emotionally disturbed children. No wonder she wanted us all to be as supportive and appreciative of the Board as possible.

But it was more difficult for me than for some of the other teachers. The Huntingtons' house, where the cocktail party would be held, was a familiar one to me. Jean Huntington was an old friend. In fact, it was she who had called me years before, when I was placement chairman for the Junior League, to suggest I look into the school for volunteer placement jobs for the members. Larry and I had gone to their house many times for dinner, as they had come to ours. I knew that our divorce had been difficult for her to understand. I knew, too, that the fact that I taught full time at the school and lived alone (except when Elizabeth and Rick were home from college), in a small apartment, seemed even more strange, more peculiar to her.

I had tried to explain it once, telling her how the children were all-absorbing to me, how their hurt and rage and fear seemed magnified versions of what I felt in all of us, how the desire to understand and do something about it drove me, making each day exciting and worthwhile, and, finally, how working at the school had changed me, had somehow stripped off my outer layers so I no longer fitted easily into her world.

I had thought Jean would understand—she was, after all, our Board Chairman and had worked hard for the school for many years—but she'd looked at me uncomprehendingly and said as gently as she could that yes, of course, she understood, but that it wasn't necessary for me to spend my whole life at it.

I had nodded, acknowledging her. There seemed to be no way to say it, but I knew that it *was* necessary, more than necessary. It was the only way that I could live, at least for now. I had lost too much time. I was too far behind. I needed to understand, to learn, to do.

The party was in full swing when I arrived. Jim Huntington greeted me at the door, saying, "Mary, how good to see you! You look marvelous. Come in."

Jean met me as I crossed the broad foyer and kissed me on the cheek. "How good of you to come. Put your coat in our bedroom. You know where it is."

"Yes," I said. "Of course. Thank you."

I could feel formality wrapping around me, covering me like plastic wrap on leftover roast. I shook my head. I had forgotten how it was, how I was.

Patty, the teacher next door to me at school, was just coming out of the master bedroom, looking clean and breezy and young in a peasant blouse and long skirt. "Boy, am I glad to see you! Something about this much class makes me nervous. How about getting out of here as soon as we can and going back to my place for a beer and some leftover stew?"

"Sounds good," I said. But I resolved to do better while I was here at the party. After all, this was a game I'd once played with ease.

Light and easy. Move and smile. Accept the drink and linger just long enough with this group. Look up. Catch an eye. Let that group move

closer. Scan the room. Someone's alone. Move to
them. Start a new group. Ah, now the talk's moving well here. Get a cigarette, accept the light. In-
quire about the children (not too deeply). Keep
it general. Underline the positive. Bright and
quick. A little laughter, not too much. Accept a
refill. Move to the right. Bend to the left.

I looked around the large, beautifully proportioned room: the Oriental rugs, the fine old ma-
hogany and cherry pieces, and the attractive,
intelligent faces, all burnished by the fire that
burned brightly in the wide fireplace. My
thoughts flickered like the fire.

I wished I'd known these people better when I
had had the chance. I wish I'd said, Talk to me
about what is important to you. Tell me your
dreams, your hopes, your sorrows. Maybe they're
the same as mine, or, if not, perhaps we can at
least understand each other. Why did I only say,
"You look great tonight. I love that color with
your tan," or, "I'll try six spades," or, "How about
being program chairman for the Cotillion?"

The Director, suddenly beside me, said, "Re-
grets?"

I turned to her, startled, but I was pleased that
she looked exactly as she always did, plain and
competent.

"No, not really. None at all about the school.
Thank you again for letting me teach there, for
hiring me. . . ."

"No business talk tonight," Jean Huntington
said, moving between us. "Have you been in to

see the tree yet? We put it up early, just for the party. It's in the library. Why don't you bring the children over from school sometime to see it?"

"Thank you," I said, thinking about the children, remembering our tree at school last year, the paper chains, the popcorn strings. I was suddenly homesick.

Patty must have sensed it. She appeared at my side from across the room. "Getting hungry?" she asked, as a maid passed a silver tray of canapes.

"How'd you know?" I answered. "I'll get my coat."

Jean followed me upstairs. What was it? Was there something she wanted to tell me? She stood quietly watching as I extracted my coat from the pile on the bed. Then she asked, "Are you still taking courses? The education courses?"

"Yes, three nights a week over at the state college."

"Oh. Well, then, you've almost got certification."

"I'm afraid not," I said. "For some reason, they're incredibly stingy with undergraduate credits, only two credits for three hours. They did give me partial credit for my two years at Wellesley, even though that was a long time ago. You were wise to finish college, Jean."

I smiled at her, remembering how long we'd known each other.

"Anyway, I need a hundred and twenty credits to graduate and I have sixty-eight so far. Even going three nights a week, I can only manage to get twelve a year, plus summer credits if I don't open the cabin for Liz and Rick. It's going to take a while."

Jean frowned. "Well, take as many as you can. . . ."

A covey of women entered the room and there was no more time to talk. I said thank you and good-bye to Jean and then hugged her. "Come see me when you can."

"I will," she promised. Something unsaid still hung in the air, but four other people were waiting impatiently to speak to her. I buttoned my coat and headed downstairs.

I sat at the table in Patty's kitchen watching her stir the stew, add more basil, and sip her beer.

"Do you like lamb stew?" she asked. I had my shoes off, my feet on another chair, and a beer of my own.

"Mm-hmm. Especially the second day. More flavor."

"Good. Me too. Listen, Mary, is it true you really lived in a house like that?"

"Sort of," I said, not wanting to talk about it, not wanting our friendship disturbed by something that had been over long ago.

"Doesn't seem possible," she said, pushing up the sleeve of her peasant blouse, amazement coloring her voice.

"Yes—well, our house wasn't quite that large."

"No," she said. "I don't mean that. Not the

house. Not the money. It's just that you don't seem old enough to live that way."

With her quick intuitive clear vision, Patty had seen through the money, through the elegance, to what was missing—vitality, excitement. She had sensed the encroachment of boredom.

I tipped my beer bottle toward her. "Thank you, Patty."

The kitchen door opened and Ted came in carrying two more six-packs. He was in his late twenties, medium height, medium build, brown hair, eyes bright behind steel-rimmed glasses. Patty and Ted lived together, saying someday, maybe someday, they might get married, but probably not; they didn't really believe in marriage. Yet it seemed to me they lived together with more love and commitment than most married couples I'd known.

Ted squeezed Patty's bottom as he went by the stove and sat down at the table inspecting me.

"Fancy duds. How was the party?"

"Okay. Fine. Not as good as here, though."

I realized as I said it that it was true. I loved the warmth and friendliness of their small kitchen. Ted was going to journalism school at Columbia and drove a cab between classes to earn money. He was warm, intelligent, and suddenly, sharply, I missed being part of a couple, part of something bigger than just one.

Patty, immediately sensitive to a mood, paused as she put the plates down on the table. "Listen, when are we going to make this a foursome? This assistant professor over at college stopped by the other night. . . ."

"No, you don't," I said. "No matchmaking. This is a single's part, at least for now."

They both nodded, accepting, not pushing me. I tried to explain a little more.

"As you two would say, I gotta get my own act together first."

13

"Of course we're going to see Santa Claus," I said. "Whoever heard of a Christmas without visiting Santa Claus?"

Friday was trip day, and our last trip before vacation was going to be a visit to Santa Claus. I had scouted the various stores and the Altman's Santa suited me best, a gentle giant of a kid, home from college, earning some extra money.

I had watched him through the late afternoon and then talked to him on his supper break, explaining about our school, our kids, wanting him to understand that they should be treated like other children, but that they might startle easily or react differently.

"Can you bring 'em in around twelve o'clock?" he asked. "Store's pretty empty then, or at least my floor is. I guess the mothers take the kids home for lunch."

His red hat, white beard, and wig were stashed on a chair beside him, his own blond hair tied back in a ponytail so that it could be stuffed up beneath the Santa Claus hat. He had taken his hamburger out of the bun and was cutting it up and eating it with a fork.

"A nose like a cherry is one hell of an inconvenience, I wanta tell you."

"You do fine," I said. "I'll bring the kids in on Friday around noon. There'll be eight children, my class and another. I haven't any idea what they'll ask for for Christmas, but whatever it is, act like it's okay. Don't give them any big reaction."

"Had a kid today, asked for a daddy. His parents had just gotten divorced."

"Mm. Well, I don't know what these kids will say. They may not want to sit on your lap, and that's okay too. It takes a little longer sometimes for them to get used to being touched."

"Hey," he said. "That doesn't sound like a bad place to go to school."

We left at ten, taking two cars. Patty had a station wagon, a volunteer, and her four kids. I had my old convertible and my four. "Meet you in the parking lot," I called to Patty as we pulled onto the highway.

Altman's was part of a large suburban shopping center approximately five miles from school. The lot was crowded with hundreds of cars of all descriptions. We tend to overbuy in suburbia to make up for something, I'm not quite sure what.

I wedged my car in beside someone who'd parked crooked and then helped the kids squeeze out through the narrow space of the half-open door. I located Patty and her group and we headed for our first stop, a toy store. I loved to

take the kids here, and they loved to go. Their
eyes grew round at the sight of so many toys.
They would have stood for hours, had there been
time, just watching the electric train run through
the make-believe village. This time Rufus and
Brian actually took turns holding the train control
by themselves—pushing the button that moved the
train forward and backward, through tunnels and
over bridges.

I watched from in front of the doll counter with
Jamie and Hannah.

"May I help you?" asked the clerk.

"Oh, sorry," I said. "I was just watching those
two boys by the train. Aren't they attractive?"

The young woman peered at Brian and Rufus.
"Look just like any other kids to me. Sorry. They
belong to you?"

"We'll take two of those doll pajama sets," I
said to reward her. Just like any other kids! I
could have kissed her ordinary face.

Jamie reached for a stuffed kitten, holding it to
his neck, cradling it, murmuring unintelligible
words.

Hannah and I surveyed the rows of dolls. I always looked for the brown-eyed Shirley Temple
doll of my childhood. I remember trying hard not
to show it was my favorite, somehow sure that
this was unfair to old stuffed Rosemary and
Nancy Lynn with the china head. Dolls had been
a large part of my early life, but it was different
for Hannah.

Impatiently, she tugged me toward the cage of

gerbils, past them to the hamsters, until we were at the cage of white mice.

"We got mices," she said. "We got lots mices home. Nice."

Mice. Rats. Bugs. These were Hannah's playmates.

"Got cat too. Cougar."

"Who?"

"Cougar. Big cat."

"Oh. I see. Cougar. And then Little Caesar."

"He Grandpa's dog. Not mine. Cougar Carl's. Not mine. But mices. They not belong anybody. They mine."

I think, I always think, my innocence is gone, that children will no longer wrench my heart—and every day I find I'm wrong.

The crowd in the store was thinning out. Eleven forty-five. I signaled Patty and the volunteer and we rounded up the kids and headed for Altman's and Santa Claus. Down the red-carpeted promenade, past the shimmering fountains into the main floor of Altman's. Tinsel, red velvet ribbon, red gift boxes tied with gold, Christmas trees of all sizes.

"Keep going," I said to Patty. "Just keep the kids moving till we get up to the fifth floor."

We headed for the elevator, but it was jammed. There was no way we could all get on and I didn't want the kids to get separated. I headed back to the escalators.

Patty stepped on the escalator holding two girls, Wanda and Barbara Lasky, by the hand.

Her volunteer followed with the other two girls. I nudged Brian and Rufus forward. "Come on, guys. You're old hands at this. Let's go." I brought up the rear with Hannah and Jamie just in front of me.

Jamie turned and buried his head against my stomach. "Turn around, Jamie. Keep your hand on the rail. That's good. I'm right here behind you." I kept one hand on his shoulder.

Santa Claus had been right; his section of the fifth floor was almost deserted. Ordinarily it was the home-decorating department, but evidently people were doing their own decorating during Christmas, and the clerks stood silently or sat in pairs talking to each other. The boys' department on the far side of the floor still seemed to have a good crowd, but Santa's spot was quiet. He sat in a wide chair on an elevated platform, talking to a tiny dark-haired girl. Only two or three children waited behind the velvet rope for their turn to speak.

We took our place in line, Rufus and Brian hurrying to be first. I stayed near them, Hannah and Jamie on either side of me. Patty's contingent was right behind us.

Rufus was very nervous when it was time for his turn, but he climbed up the three steps to the platform. He wasn't going to sit on any lap, though. He surveyed Santa through his horn-rimmed glasses from the edge of the platform.

"What's your name, sonny?"

"It's not sonny."

"Sorry."

"My father says there isn't any Santa Claus, so I don't believe in you. I'm Jewish anyway, and we don't believe in Christmas. We have Hanukkah; we have candles and twelve days and I don't believe in Santa Claus."

Poor Santa. He was a little taken aback, but he held his own. He handed Rufus a balloon full of paper snowflakes and said, "Listen, fella. Don't worry about it. Lots of people don't believe in anything at all any more, much less Christmas. Happy holiday. Who's next? Okay. Come on up here, fella. What's your name?"

Brian's hands were beating a rapid tattoo against his sides. "Brian," he said. "Brian O'Connell ... rat-a-tat ... boom boom ba ... our next contestant will be ... what's your name?"

When Brian was scared or nervous, hundreds of thoughts and sentences crowded through his head and he couldn't keep them all inside, although he tried, cutting them off in midsentence, trying to hold to one line of thought.

"Eh? What'd you say? Er—my name? Er, my name is Santa Claus. Heh-heh."

Santa was getting a little nervous himself and he glanced down at me for support. I signaled A-okay. His wasn't an easy job.

Brian ripped off three commercials and then finally asked for an Eldorado, a wardrobe designed exclusively by Bill Blass, and a week's vacation at a Club Mediterranee.

"Oh, boy," said Santa Claus, looking at me.

"You didn't tell me, lady. You didn't half tell me. How many more we got?"

"Six," I said.

"Six? Kee-rist! Excuse me—sweet Jesus of Bethlehem. Okay, lady, let's go. Let's get 'em up here to see ol' jolly Santa."

Barbara Lasky crowded by and massaged his face and beard, saying, "Look what you did to your hair. Oh-h-h, look what you did to your hair." She didn't ask for anything.

Tina sat on his lap and promised to be a good, good girl all year and not take her clothes off on the bus and then requested a new neon sign to play with Vacuum Cleaner. Wanda Gomez was the best of all and asked for a new doll and a necklace just like her teacher's, and she didn't bite her arm at all. Beautiful Jane refused to go up on the platform, laughing silently beside the volunteer.

"Only two more now," I said encouragingly.

Hannah went up slowly, standing right in front of Santa Claus.

"Got list," she said.

"Got lost?" asked Santa hopefully.

"No," said Hannah clearly. "List. Christmas list. Read now. Okay, Santa Claus?"

"Yeah, sure. You bet. Anything you say, sweetheart. Go ahead."

Hannah, standing straight before him in her blue sailor dress, took a crumpled piece of paper out of her pocket and read, "Christmas List for

Santa Claus, by Hannah. New stove—Mama. Gun
—Carl. New lamp—Grandpa. Ball—Baby Helen.
Cheese—Mices."

"Okay, everybody. Hold it just where you are."
A photographer had suddenly materialized out of
nowhere. "We'll get a lovely picture for your folks,
little girl. You'll treasure it forever," the man said,
looking at me.

"No," I said. "Don't do that!" But before I
could stop him he held up a camera: flash—click!

Chaos.

Hannah burst into tears and Jamie leaped like a
thunderbolt, away under the red velvet rope and
across the store. I was after him immediately,
walking casually but fast, out through the decorating department, on by the escalator over to the
other side of the store, into the boys' department.

Jamie was wearing his bright blue jacket with
white lettering and his blue baseball cap, so I
could pick him out easily. There weren't many
kids his size in the store anyway, school was still
in session, and the ones that were there sure
weren't wearing baseball caps in midwinter.

Jamie stopped by the glove counter and looked
back to see what was happening. I made a quick
move behind a Christmas tree, but either it was
too small or I was too slow. Anyway, he spotted
me. To his delight.

The clerk at the glove counter said, "Can I help
you, little boy?"

Jamie ducked and headed away from the

counter. I followed as closely and discreetly as I could. I couldn't leave him here alone, but I knew Jamie from his early runaway days at the school and I also knew I couldn't chase him. There is nothing a runaway likes more than having someone chase him. Then he's the one in control.

Casually I walked among the lady shoppers, turning a glove, touching a scarf. I was getting a little closer now. Maybe everything would be all right. I stopped by the hat table, a large wooden rectangle set up in the middle of the floor. I turned a Norwegian knit cap over and then glanced up. Jamie was directly opposite me on the other side.

"Hey there, Jamie," I mouthed more than spoke and took one step to my left.

Jamie immediately took one step to his left as well, keeping the same exact distance between us. His eyes were dazed. I wasn't at all sure he recognized me. I took four more small quick steps, which brought me around the corner of my side to the end of the table.

Jamie took four equally quick steps, which brought him to his end of the table. We were exactly opposite each other again, and we were beginning to have a lot of clear space in which to move. The shoppers, well-dressed suburbanite mothers and matrons, were drawing back, moving away. They sensed something was going on and paused to observe.

Jamie and I were alone at the table—except for

perhaps thirty or forty women who lined the sidelines two feet away. I moved. He moved.

"Hullo, Jamie. Hey there, now."

No answer. His eyes were the bright staring eyes of a trapped animal.

For one second I thought, What am I doing here in this crazy silent ballet in front of these women? How come I'm not just there watching too?

In that one second, a man dressed in a dark blue suit managed to get beside me. "Do you have a little problem?" he inquired unctuously.

"No, I have a little boy," I replied furiously. "Go away." I knew Jamie would get more upset if there was a stranger there.

"I'm sorry, madam. What goes on in this department is my responsibility. I cannot go away. I'm the department manager. What's the matter with your little boy? Is he tired and hungry? We have lots of tired, hungry children these days. Mothers should know better. Ha-ha. Take them home earlier."

I thought I might hit him, but I needn't have bothered. Jamie thought of it first.

A fur-lined hat sailed across the table and struck the department manager on the arm. A gasp went up from the watching ladies.

"Oh, my, now, young fellow. You shouldn't have done that. Well, madam, I'm sorry, but I'm just going to have to step in and take charge. . . ."

"I wouldn't do that," I began, but the manager

was in full tilt now, chasing Jamie around the table. Jamie kept the same distance between them with no trouble at all, chucking hats all the time he moved.

"Stop that now." Anger and impatience mounted in the manager's voice. "Just you stop that, you bad boy."

I had to do something. The store was a mess, the table a heap of confusion; hats were all over the floor. Jamie was capable of much more. I had seen him sink his teeth deep into a teacher's arm two years before.

The manager turned to the crowd. "All right," he whined angrily. "Call the guards. Get them up here right away."

I wasn't sure what I was doing, but I had to do something and it wasn't going to be at the hat table. Jamie had already staked out that territory.

I walked as slowly as I could toward the escalator. I took long, slow, loud, definite steps. I never looked back. Finally I said, low but clear, with absolute certainty, "Lunchtime, Jamie. Let's get back to school."

I kept walking. I didn't turn my head. I reached the top of the escalator and I stopped. There was nowhere else to go. I could see Patty and the volunteer with the other children at the bottom. Hannah was in the front of the group, peering worriedly up the moving steps. The store was completely silent. I stood still, thinking once again, What am I doing here? Who do I think I am?

Then I felt a small hand touch my right hand. Small and hot and wet. I looked down and there was Jamie, standing quiet, standing close, his hand in mine.

"Hey there, Jamie," I said—and I knew what I was doing there. I knew who I was.

14

I finished my last exam at eight o'clock the night of December twenty-third, picked up the Christmas turkey and an extra box of lights for the tree, and made it home just ten minutes before Elizabeth and Rick arrived. They were full of news of their colleges, interested in my education courses, and we talked almost nonstop for two days. The day after Christmas we flew to Florida, the plane fare my major Christmas present to them. We stayed with good, longtime friends. The weather was warm and full of sunshine and the rest of the days and nights blurred together and were over far too soon.

Elizabeth and Rick flew directly back to school from Florida. I arrived home late the night of January first and tumbled into bed without bothering to unpack or do more than glance at the mail.

The alarm jangled me awake the next morning, just in time for school. The luxury of vacation and slow awakenings was over, but by the time I was in the car and on my way to school, I was wide awake and eager to see the kids again.

But later on I wasn't so sure. The morning had been a disaster. The first day back after any vacation is usually difficult, but today had been even worse than usual. Circle had been chaotic. Patty's class had jabbered senselessly while Hannah refused to talk or sing at all. Back in our room, at the end of Best and Worst, Hannah burst into tears and told her story. No Best. Only Worst.

She had gotten cheese for her mice for Christmas—Santa forgot. She had named the mice Wynken, Blynken, and Nod and made a house for them from a box and scraps of cloth. But Christmas night Cougar had killed them. Carl had deliberately put Cougar in Hannah's room after she was asleep, and during the night Cougar killed Wynken and Blynken and ate Nod, leaving only his head.

No wonder Hannah was upset. It was too much. She had tried to salvage some joy from her meager life—having no friends, she had tried to make the mice her companions and even these had been killed by her brother's cat. Where was the sunshine now? Where was Hannah's share? Who deals out life, anyway? How come some people get such crummy cards each time?

I rocked Hannah after we had finished Best and Worst. This was no day for reading.

At lunch Patty said, "What did you think of the letter from the Board?"

I put down my coffee cup. "What letter?"

"Nothing special. Just the form letter they enclosed in their Christmas card. It had a little sketch of the new school and a few paragraphs describing the kitchen, the central swimming pool, the staff of certified teachers, all made possible by state funding. I just wondered if it affected you." Patty's tone was unconcerned.

"I don't know," I said. "I don't think so. Nobody's said anything."

That afternoon things were almost as bad as in the morning, and every teacher in the school, including me, was eager for the day to end.

Jamie, the last to leave, was just getting on his bus when Zoe, our secretary, came in from the office.

"You've got a visitor. Want me to say you've gone?"

"Who is it?"

"Mrs. Rosnic."

"Mrs. Rosnic? Hannah just left. What's she doing here? Who's going to take care of Hannah?"

"Don't ask me. She was halfway to your room when I stopped her and took her back to the office."

I followed Zoe out of my room.

Mrs. Rosnic stood by the office door looking dumpy and pale and scared in her worn black coat, turning the handle of her large black purse nervously between her hands.

"Hello," I said, touching her arm. "Let's go down to my room."

Zoe's intentions were good, I was anxious to get home, but still it was essential for Mrs. Rosnic, for all the parents, to have easy access to my room. I rarely made what the Director called "house visits," those unexpected stops to the children's homes. Many teachers did and the Director encouraged it, but I had tried once and found a mother with a swollen lip and bruised eye and a sinkful of dishes. She had apologized, mumbling something about her husband having tied one on the night before, and her embarrassment and humiliation were so deep that she couldn't talk about her child. The Director pointed out that I had learned quite a bit, but to me it was prying and I wanted no part of it. So I encouraged the parents to come to school without making appointments. They all came often, and it was important that they feel welcome during their visits.

Now Mrs. Rosnic began to talk before we even got back to the room, saying Grandpa was taking care of the children, telling about Carl, Hannah, the mice, the cat. Telling how Hannah had refused to wash or change her clothes all vacation, throwing tantrums, kicking at the thin walls, yelling, screaming, two or three times a day.

The neighbors had complained to the police. Grandpa wanted Hannah put away. Mrs. Rosnic was at the end of her rope.

I walked around the room, trying to think, trying to get perspective, to see it from Mrs. Rosnic's point of view. Hannah's stories hung on every wall I passed—she could read now, she could write, she was willing to talk. I was so proud of her. And yet, what good was this if she couldn't live in her own home? What did any of it matter if her behavior was so bad, so uncontrolled, that it drove her out of her house into an institution? While Hannah had learned to control her behavior in school, she still used tantrums to get her own way at home. Mrs. Rosnic and I had discussed this before, particularly during the days of blue dessert, but evidently I hadn't been specific enough.

I went back to Mrs. Rosnic. "Let's sit down."

Mrs. Rosnic kept on talking. "What she care about mice for? Plenty more where they come from."

On Mrs. Rosnic's block mice and poverty were part of life. No one had mice for pets but Hannah. Everyone considered them problems and struggled to cope with them. But no one had a child like Hannah. Her tantrums, her screams and shouted gibberish, were evidence to the neighbors that here was a "queer kid," some kind of "loony"—a "retard." This was what was unbearable to Mrs. Rosnic. This was what was important to her.

"Now she say she no go to school. Never. She not care what I say. This morning I yell and yell at her, tell her hurry, bus almost here. Carl laugh, tell her she be late for Circle at retard school. Hannah scream, hit him. Then Grandpa come up, get her, hold her, and I get dress on—and finally we get her on bus."

Who could blame Hannah, hurt and angry over the loss of her cherished mice, lonely in the midst of despair? Who could blame Grandpa and Mrs. Rosnic, humiliated, ostracized by the neighbors because of Hannah's behavior, longing for a few hours of peace and quiet, willing to buy it at any cost? How could you even blame Carl, taking out his own anger on his sister? Never mind blame. What counted was not losing Hannah. She was doing well in school; she could do even better. But I needed more time.

"Listen," I said to Mrs. Rosnic. "You're going to have to let her yell for a couple of days. Talk to your neighbors. Explain that it will be hard for a day or two, but then it will be better."

"Yell? She already yell. What do you mean yell?"

"I mean that right now Hannah gets whatever she wants, or doesn't want, by yelling and throwing a tantrum. You and Grandpa hate to have her yell, so you give in or else have a big scene and force her, which pleases her almost as much. Hannah wants your attention, needs it badly, but she shouldn't be getting it by yelling."

"She yell, all right," Mrs. Rosnic said, nodding, not seeming to comprehend what I was saying, though she was listening closely. "What I do? What you say for me to do when she yell?"

"Let her yell some more."

I could see dread and understanding beginning to come in Mrs. Rosnic's eyes.

"For instance, when she yells about not coming to school, don't pay any attention to her. If she misses the bus, let her miss it."

There was silence in our room. Then Mrs. Rosnic said, "Let her stay home all day? Not make her go to school? All day let her yell if she want?"

"That's right. It won't hurt her. She has to learn that yelling doesn't change anything."

Mrs. Rosnic was mute.

I could see her not wanting to relinquish those six hours of relative peace when Hannah was away. But she was a strong woman and I was counting on her strength and the fact that she loved Hannah and that underneath it all Hannah really did love school.

"Lay out Hannah's school clothes," I said. "Wake her up forty-five minutes before the bus is due. Tell her to get up, get washed, get dressed. Then leave her alone and don't go back no matter what, not if she stays in bed, not if she screams her head off.

"Go on to the kitchen and make breakfast. Make something that Hannah likes to eat and that you enjoy making. But choose something easy and cheap, so that you can throw it out if she doesn't eat it. When there's fifteen minutes left before the bus comes, call Hannah for breakfast. If she's ready, praise her! Feed her! But if she isn't, don't go to her room. Let her bus come and go. Throw out the breakfast. Let her stay home.

"Hannah is eight years old, Mrs. Rosnic. She should have been dressing herself, getting ready for school, doing all these things on her own for years now."

I knew I sounded tough, but I had to. It was

going to be hard for Mrs. Rosnic to stand up to Hannah, but it was the only way that Hannah would be able to remain at home, away from the institution.

I am no Skinnerian, thinking that people can be trained to dance like pigeons for birdseed or a few M and M's. It's a mechanical view that denies the creative, loving soul of man—but still, we all thrive on approval, and if we can't get the approval, we'll settle for attention. A child like Hannah can become a tyrant, making the lives around her miserable and her own life impossible. The only thing to do when this happens is to get rid of the bad behavior, gradually but surely.

Sometimes there's an even more vicious cycle. A parent will vaguely realize that he's being manipulated. He resolves not to pay attention; the child then tunes up his bad behavior and screams louder or does something even worse until his parent decides that *this* is too much, he can't let *this* go on, so he no longer ignores and the child again has the attention. As time goes on, the child's behavior becomes increasingly worse and the parent increasingly frustrated. The only way out of this double bind is totally and completely to ignore the bad and praise the tiniest good.

Mrs. Rosnic sighed and stood up. "Grandpa, he won't like it."

"Hannah's going to like it even less," I said. "Call me if I can help."

I read the letter from the Board when I got

home. Patty was right; that was what it said. The Board was proud to announce the fall opening of the new building, complete with ten classrooms, carpeting, bathrooms adjacent to each classroom, a large, fully equipped kitchen and lunchroom, a central heated swimming pool—and a fully certified staff.

Fully certified. It would be several years before I had certification. I thought about it in the shower and during dinner and before I fell asleep. All night long I dreamed of swimming pools and mice and certifications. Cougar ate Hannah by mistake, leaving only her head, while I chased a spider-legged, black, framed certificate down a snowy road.

I took the Board's letter to school the next morning and pointed to the words "fully certified" as I asked the Director, "Does that include me, do you think? Or will they give me provisional certification for my experience and the courses I'm taking?"

The Director was busy and vague. "It's hard to tell what the Board means. Why they put so much stock in those courses, I don't know. Well, I suppose it's the state laws. I just don't know what's going to happen. It's up to the Board. . . .

"Mary, I'm due at a meeting in Milton. The neighbors have signed a petition against the new school. They say they're afraid to have 'crazy children' on their block. Even at this late date, there's a chance they can still stop us. I just don't have time to talk to you now."

The phone rang. It was Mrs. Gomez: Wanda's bus driver hadn't come yet, was over thirty minutes late. Then Henry came in to say the furnace was out. I went on down to my classroom as confused as when I'd arrived.

Hannah didn't come in at all that day. She was absent the next day as well, with no word from Mrs. Rosnic. I waited, or tried to wait, reminding myself that teachers often forget how well mothers and fathers know their children. Teachers forget the hours parents spend holding, feeding, touching, playing, bathing, caring for the child when he's sick, knowing sounds and smells and intricacies that a teacher can never know.

By Thursday afternoon I wasn't able to think about anything but Hannah. "If she's not in by tomorrow morning, I'm going to have to call," I told the Director after school.

"Do you want me to call now?" the Director asked.

"No," I said. "Mrs. Rosnic has my number at home, as well as this one. I'm sure she'd call if something was wrong."

But would she? Who did I think I was, anyway, telling her what to do? Hannah had survived for eight years without my advice. Maybe I'd made things worse instead of better.

Friday morning was raw and cold, and it seemed to me that this had been the longest week in history. I arrived early, so did the boys, but none of us mentioned Hannah. Jamie started the record player and with one foot in front of the other began rocking back and forth, back and forth.

I went to divert him, and just then Hannah walked in, and we all yelled together, "Hannah! Hello!"

Hannah ignored us completely and went straight to the closet. Oh, dear God, I thought. Please not that again. Please let's not have to begin all over from the coat closet.

But Hannah stayed there only a minute, just long enough to hang up her coat. From there she went directly to her cubby and began taking inventory, laying the crayons, pencils, books on the floor, ignoring us completely. The boys and I watched, mesmerized.

Finally Brian couldn't stand it any longer and went and squatted beside her in front of her cubby.

"Hey, Hannah, where you been? We missed ... boom-boom ... we didn't know ... what happened to you?"

Hannah arranged her books neatly in the cupboard, taking her time, choosing her minute, making it plain that she was her own woman. No matter what had happened, Hannah was going to tell it her way and make it stick.

At last she looked at Brian and then said coolly and with great dignity, "Nothing happen. I just decide take little extra vacation."

And that was all she ever said about those three days.

Now, to my delight Mrs. Rosnic began to come to the Wednesday mothers' groups. She, who had never had time before, came to the meetings now. She, who couldn't drive in traffic, drove now. She, who had never been able to be separated from baby Helen, left her without a qualm with the other younger brothers and sisters in the nursery while she, Mrs. Rosnic, no longer inarticulate, no longer shy, told how she had trained Hannah to be ready on time each day for the bus driver, told how she had outlasted Hannah's tantrums. The other mothers listened, impressed, and then asked questions, and Mrs. Rosnic answered and told them how.

15

"Who knows what a play is?" I asked.

"Play is have fun," Hannah answered immediately. "Play ball, like that."

"Okay. That's good. That's one meaning of play. Anybody know another? Suppose I said we're going to see a play? What would that mean?"

"Like on television," Brian said. "They have plays on television ... interrupted by only four commercials. Boom boom. 'This original screenplay is brought to you by Hallmark.' "

"Yeah. Right. No commercials now, though."

"Is it a movie, Mary?" Rufus asked. "Like something in New York? On my mother's birthday last year they went to a play in New York."

"Yup. There are lots of plays in New York. And it's like a movie, only better. The people are real—just like us—walking around, talking, acting out a story. And what do you think? We're going to go to a play ourselves. You, and you, and you, and you. And me. We're all going to see a play a week from today. Not in New York, but right here—over at Wilson Memorial School."

Every year the Children's Theater group of the

155

Junior League put on a play for children. It was a high-quality production, representing many hours of work and much talent. The Junior Leaguers made up the costume committee, the scenery committee, the program committee, and the publicity committee, as well as the cast. They spent many long hours of rehearsal directed by a professional director hired and brought out from New York. Rehearsals ran from September through the fall and early winter; then, from late January to March, they trouped the play to a dozen elementary schools throughout the area, bringing live theater to children without charge. This year's play was *Pinocchio* and I had gotten permission for us to go see it at the local school.

Each day after lunch I read the story of Pinocchio to the children, so that they would be familiar with fat, kind Gepetto, the beautiful Blue Fairy, Pinocchio and his nose that grew longer with each lie, and Lampwick, the bad boy. I was sure the play would be different from the book, but still I thought the children would follow it better if they had a general idea of the characters.

The Director and the kids' parents had both given permission for the trip. The principal of Wilson Memorial School was more difficult. I had encountered the same kind of evasiveness before. We were not what you would call a popular group. Other kinds of schools, other groups of children, are welcome at all sorts of places and on all kinds of tours. But emotionally disturbed children are not welcome anywhere. In the beginning we could slip in and out without notice, but now as our school became more well known in public as well as professional circles and was highlighted in newspaper articles, it was more difficult.

What were they so afraid of, I wondered? If the worst should happen and one of the kids should blow his cool, it wouldn't be the end of the world. However, there was no way of convincing public officials of this, so mainly I just agreed to whatever promises they exacted and then dealt with problems as they came along.

This principal had said the only empty seats for the performance were in the front row. If he thought this would scare us off, he was wrong. I agreed immediately, so then he decided that actually the only available seats were in the last row, but I allowed as how we'd stick with the first row. Then he wanted to be sure we could make ourselves small enough so that the other children could see over us. Absolutely. If he'd asked if we could make ourselves invisible, I would have assured him of that as well.

Actually, when we arrived there were plenty of empty seats, as I expected. We sat front row center, but there was a full empty row behind us plus more at the sides.

We got there early; the stage curtain was still closed. I sat between Jamie and Hannah, with Rufus on one end and Brian on the other. They were all quiet, awed by the vastness of the auditorium—the room was more than four times the size of any at our school. I could feel Hannah's arm trembling against my own. As the children marched in in single file, Brian leaned across to ask if this was what "regular" school was like.

Then the heavy draperies were pulled across the high screened windows, the lights went out, and the curtain went up.

It was marvelous. We all—old, young, teacher, student, regular and emotionally disturbed—gasped together to see Pinochhio there, looking just as he did in the book, stiff and wooden with painted cheeks and a pointed cap. And there was Gepetto, too, old and fat in a leather apron, kind, doing everything for Pinocchio, who obviously was a very naughty boy and didn't appreciate Gepetto's kindness at all.

I looked away from the stage at my four children, all on the edges of their seats, leaning forward, forgetting to make themselves small. And I didn't remind them—they had been small long enough.

Now here came the Blue Fairy. She didn't have blue hair as she did in the book, but she was dressed in a short frothy blue tulle ballet costume with a jeweled tiara and a sparkling wand. She glittered and twirled, pirouetted and performed her magic.

Beside me Hannah sighed. "Is beautiful."

When the play was over we cheered and clapped with the rest of the children as the cast took its curtain calls, and then sat silently as the principal belatedly welcomed us.

On the way back to school, Rufus and Brian chattered like magpies. How had Pinocchio turned into a real boy? How had he made his nose grow? I smiled, happy with the success of the trip.

"So you liked the play," I said.

"Yeah," Rufus answered. "Listen, Mary. Listen, you kids. You know what? I bet we could make a play. All you have to do is write down words for people to say. I could do that, I bet. And get some things to wear. You could do that, Mary. See, we could do a play just like that Pinocchio—and have the other kids at school come see it."

Brian loved the idea. "And we can have commercials—"

Rufus said before I could, "Naah, Brian. We don't need any dumb commercials. But see, I can be Pinocchio. You can be Lampwick. Ah, Gepetto—"

Hannah said quickly, "I be Gepetto."

"Yeah," Rufus said. "That'd be good. You're sort of—"

But Gepetto was old and fat and homely. That's not the way I wanted Hannah to see herself. I knew who she had thought was beautiful.

"What about Jamie?" I asked. "He'd be good as Gepetto."

But Rufus said, "Mary, Gepetto talks a lot. He says more than anybody."

Rufus was right. That wouldn't work. I'd have to try another tack.

"Well, listen then. Let Jamie be Lampwick. Lampwick doesn't talk much."

"Well," said Rufus. "Maybe. . . ."

"Will you make costumes, Mary?" Brian wanted to know.

"We'll all help with the costumes. We can do it in the afternoons." There went another science project, but I didn't care. They could learn about magnets next year.

Come on. Come on, I thought. Who's going to mention the Blue Fairy? Hurry up, Rufus. Brian, help him. Come on now. You volunteer to be Gepetto—let Hannah be the Blue Fairy. Make it your idea.

"Well, all right," said slow, deliberate Rufus. "But if Jamie's Lampwick, who's gonna be the fairy? You need a girl for the fairy. . . ."

Brian's sweet, reedy voice piped up. "Hannah. She's a girl. She can be the Blue Fairy."

Good, Brian.

"Yeah, well, but she's . . ." Rufus hesitated, not wanting to be unkind. Our children were rarely unkind to each other if they weren't angry.

"That'd be great," I confirmed. "What do you say, lovey? Rufus will be Pinocchio and Jamie, Lampwick; you let Brian be Gepetto and you be the Blue Fairy."

Hannah sat absolutely still, looking straight ahead. She closed her eyes as if to visualize that dancing, shimmering, shining image of loveliness. She opened her eyes again and still didn't speak. Then finally she took a big breath. "Okay," she said. "I let you be Gepetto, Bri-an. I be Blue Fairy."

We wrote our play; it was twenty pages long and I typed it up carefully and read it back to the children. Then I typed out scripts for everybody, but nobody except Brian could learn his part and they got more mixed up trying to read them. So finally we threw the scripts away and concentrated on the costumes and the scenery, and everyone said what came into his head at the time.

We practiced every afternoon for two weeks and finally on a Wednesday morning, the first week of February, we were ready.

There was an unused room next to Patty's, separated from hers by a wooden folding door. It was used, on occasion, by the church as a small chapel. For our play, we pushed back the door and Henry, gaunt, never smiling, but gentle, careful with his hands, helped us put up the painted cardboard for scenery and arrange the chairs for the rest of the school.

The play opened with Brian as Gepetto teaching Rufus how to walk, helping him to move his stiff wooden legs. Gepetto sold his coat to buy Pinocchio a spelling book, so he could go to school. Brian loved this part and kept patting his leather apron and sneaking in commercials. On the way to school Pinocchio met up with Lampwick—Jamie rocked across the stage in excitement, grabbed Pinocchio, and led him to the Land of Pleasure without having to say a word.

Then Pinocchio told his first lie and then another and another and his nose (an empty toilet paper roll with a paper cone inside) grew longer and our whole school clapped and cheered—and my kids got so excited that they all ran off the stage and Henry had to herd them back on. It was time for the Blue Fairy to appear and help Pinocchio.

Hannah had stayed hidden behind one of the window curtains, but now, as Henry whispered to her, she ran out onto the stage. Mrs. Rosnic had made her a beautiful costume out of old sheets. It was longer than that of the Junior League's Blue Fairy, but it was dyed a soft deep blue so that Hannah's own eyes seemed even bluer.

Her wand was the end of an old fishing rod with an aluminum star at the end. Her tiara balanced precariously on her short, gleaming hair. She looked better than I had ever seen her, but, she wasn't doing anything. Even Jamie had managed to run out on the stage and grab Rufus to lead him to the Land of Pleasure. But Hannah did nothing, and the awkward pause grew longer and longer as Rufus shifted from foot to foot, waiting for the Blue Fairy to touch his long nose with her wand and make it short again. (Rufus was supposed to poke the cone of paper back inside the toilet paper roll as he reached up in delight to touch his shortened nose.)

This was to have been the high point of the show—and now Hannah stood doing nothing while Rufus glowered at her and Brian whispered,

"Go on, Hannah. Touch his nose with the star. You can do it."

But Hannah didn't budge.

Rufus was getting angrier and angrier. "Hurry up," he hissed. "Hurry up, dummy."

That did it. Hannah wasn't going to be called dummy by anybody, any more. She moved immediately across the stage, up to the impatient Pinocchio. She forgot about being the Blue Fairy, forgot Pinocchio, forgot the play and the audience.

Whack! Down came the wand on Rufus's paper nose—hard, as hard as Hannah could bring it down.

"Not dummy," shouted the Blue Fairy. "I not dummy any more. Not call me that."

Pinocchio's nose rolled across the stage. Rufus's own nose had barely escaped the blow, and now it looked small and vulnerable in his painted face. Our play was a shambles, or I thought it was, but the children didn't. They'd never seen a play before, never heard of Pinocchio, and they loved the action and excitement of what was going on.

I picked up Pinocchio's nose so it wouldn't be stepped on and handed it to Gepetto, who was the closest.

Brian took the nose, his hands flapping just a little with excitement, and with inspiration he went center stage. "Good beautiful Blue Fairy. You have saved Pinocchio. You got rid of his horrible nose and gave him the wonderful nose of a real boy. We thank you. The End. Brought to you by General Electric, the Wonderful House of Magic."

We all stood and cheered. Rufus and Hannah forgot to be mad and cheered too. Even Jamie clapped his hands. Our play was a hit, a four-star hit.

Who says you need a script?

16

"Oh, boy, teacher," Hannah said. "You not even know it Valentine's Day. Oh, boy."

"I'm sorry. I forgot all about it."

"That okay. Not matter. I got two presents."

"Two presents?"

Hannah nodded vigorously. "Two. One from me. One from Mama."

"For me?" I asked. "Two for me? Oh, Hannah. I don't have any."

"That okay, teacher. We got two. Here. Open."

In Hannah's mind it didn't matter who got the presents or who gave them as long as there were the same number of presents as people.

"The world has got a lot to learn from you, lovey."

She cocked her head at me quizzically, not understanding, not really caring, too excited about her presents.

"Here," she said, handing me a brown paper bag. "Open. From Mama."

I reached into the bag and took out a foil-wrapped package. I folded back the edges of the foil and found a loaf of bread on a paper plate with a note.

You teach her good. Happy Valentine's Day—Mrs. Rosnic.

The loaf was brown and crisp and round.

"That's beautiful bread!" I said. "Your mom is a good cook. Thank you, Hannah. It's really beautiful."

"That not mine. This mine. Look."

"You're right," I said. "I'll write your mother tonight."

Hannah handed me an even bigger paper bag with a long roll of paper sticking out the top of the bag.

"Open," Hannah urged.

I slit the tape that held the roll together and spread the paper out on the table while Hannah said, "I paint that, teacher."

It was a lovely, happy picture with a strong blue sky and a large yellow sun. Below the sun was a figure dancing. It wore a skirt and—could those be sneakers?

"Sneakers?" I asked.

Hannah nodded and confirmed, "Sneakers. That how you look sometimes. And see, here your heart."

My heart? Could Hannah see my heart? Had anybody ever seen my heart? I could hear it now—*boom boom boom*. Had anybody ever even wanted to see my heart before? But there it was on Hannah's picture, a big red blob on the outside.

"That's nice, Hannah," I said. "That's a nice heart."

"It big, teacher. It a big heart."

I put my hands under her armpits and lifted her plump, sturdy little body up onto the table so that her eyes were level with mine, and put my arms around her, hugging her hard.

"Not half as big as yours, lovey. Not half."

17

"All right, Mary. I'll stick my neck out and make it definite. There'll be a sure spot for Brian at P.S. 24 next fall; I'll see to it. You've done a good job with him." Bernie Sorrino, Regional Director of Special Services, turned suddenly to me and said, "Who'm I kidding? You've done a lot more than that. It's some kind of a miracle, what's happened to that kid. I remember him when we sent him to you, weirdest kid I ever saw, didn't eat, didn't talk, flapped and squawked around like some crazy kinda bird."

"Thanks, Bernie. You won't be sorry. He'll do you proud," I said.

"Yeah. Well, we'll see. I've promised to take him, and I won't go back on my word. But by God, Mary, you better toughen him up between now and then or those city kids will eat him alive."

The Director of Special Services was right and I knew it. Bernie was a tough, smart, honest man who had worked his way up out of the slums of the city himself. He'd scrounged and scratched, won or wangled one scholarship after another, until he'd finally gotten his doctorate in education.

He had started in surburban schools; when I first knew him he was in charge of special services for the whole northwestern section of our state, an area that is affluent, sophisticated, and relatively serene. Five years ago he had been asked to take over special services in the teeming, run-down, industrial city where both he and Brian had been born, more than forty years apart. In fact, he was there before he was asked, applying for the job that wasn't even open yet.

Our Director had disapproved of his move. "I thought Bernie had a good head on his shoulders. He was moving right along, but if he goes back to the city now, he'll never get out again. He won't get those kind of breaks twice."

Bernie came up to our school three or four times a year to check on Brian, the only child we'd ever had from the city. The Superintendent of Schools had told our Director tersely, "We take care of our own." But they couldn't take care of Brian. They had tried him in their public schools, in their retarded classes, on home instruction. Eventually, on Brian's father's plea, they had grudgingly sent him to us four years ago, when he was eight years old. I could understand some of their reluctance; they had no school bus for special education and yet state law said they must provide transportation. So Brian traveled the twenty miles back and forth to our school in a taxi every day, not an easy thing to explain to the city taxpayers.

I'd liked Bernie Sorrino from the beginning.

When he came to visit he really came into the classroom; no hanging on the edges or peeping in the windows for Bernie. If we were at Circle, he opened the door, dragged over one of the small chairs, and plopped himself down next to one of the kids, his bulk extending beyond the small chair seat, his short, strong legs sticking out into the circle. He was far from inconspicuous, but there was something natural, easy, and ebullient about him, so that his visits were always welcome. He sang whatever we were singing in an unself-conscious, off-key voice, and the kids accepted him far more easily than they did the timid visitors who tiptoed around the room, trying to make themselves inconspicuous. Bernie never peered purposefully at Brian or took "little notes—just to refresh my mind," as many of the administrators or social workers or psychologists did. But when he'd been there about an hour he'd signal with his head and I'd follow him into the hall.

On his first visit to the school he lit a cigar as soon as we hit the hall, puffed on it for a minute, staring into space, then turned back to me. "Oh, sorry—forgot. You want one?" Proffering a big fat cigar.

"No, thanks." I was waiting. I couldn't tell yet. Was he joking? Was he testing?

"That kid," he continued. "That kid I'm here to see, Brian O'Connell—how's he doing?"

"Okay. He's come a long way; he's got a long way to go."

"All right, Mary." He knew my name; obviously

he knew far more than he let on. "I want him reading by the next time I come. Got that?" His eyes, black and prominent behind the cigar smoke, crackled.

"Absolutely," I said, straight-faced but feeling good. "The whole encyclopedia, right?"

Bernie Sorrino glared back, clapping me on the shoulder with a strong, warm hand. "*And* the World Book. Don't forget the World Book, for Christ's sake."

That had been four years ago. We'd liked each other then. We liked each other even better now. I'd been on a couple of panels on childhood schizophrenia and autism with him. Once he'd worn his wife's name tag by mistake all through a public session—and he thought it as funny as the audience did when I pointed it out to him.

But I took Bernie seriously now. He knew Brian, and he knew the city. If he said to toughen him up, it was something that had to be done.

I walked with Bernie out to the car, the kids following, then passing us on their bikes. "Can you give me some more specifics?" I asked. "How am I going to toughen him up?"

"Teach him to lie, cheat, steal, roll dice, play poker, drink, deal drugs, use a knife, indulge in a little rape, and keep his skin intact. For Christ's sake, now you got him singing about Noah and his arkie-ark and Puff the Magic Dragon. Jesus, Mary, what good's that gonna do him in the city?"

This was legitimate criticism. The atmosphere

of our school was warm, protective, loving. We dealt with reality, but a reality of our own. We faced wide ranges of emotion and behavior with equanimity. We replaced fantasy and escapism with immediacy. Our purpose was to build, encourage, promote trust and openness among the children and the staff so that warm interpersonal relationships could (and did) develop.

Brian was a good product of our school; he was open, without guile, tender, trusting—but vulnerable, an easy target. The reality of our classroom was far different from that of P.S. 24. As I thought about it more, it became clear that we were innocent and protective in a way that would be detrimental to Brian.

But if the problem was clear, the solution wasn't. Who was going to teach him? Not Jamie, Hannah, or Rufus—and I didn't know much more.

I brought a deck of cards and some poker chips to school the next day. I slit the cellophane on the poker chips and said to the kids, "Okay, we got a new game here. It's called five-card stud." I had to start somewhere, and I knew a little more about cards than the other items that Bernie had mentioned. I said to Brian, "This is mainly for you. They'll be playing cards at your school next year."

Brian smiled. "Like Concentration? I like Concentration."

"No, Bri. Not like that. Not like that at all." It

was true that Brian loved Concentration, both the
card game and the television show. He had a fantastic visual memory; he knew all the states and
capitals, baseball players and batting averages.
He could remember card sequences and positions
with no effort at all. He would be able to learn
poker without any trouble. But that wasn't the
point. I had to try to set him up. I wasn't going to
teach him to cheat, but I was going to try to show
him what to do when somebody else did.

Brian caught on to poker quickly; Rufus perse-
vered; Jamie and Hannah soon lost interest.

Three-handed poker isn't the best game in the
world, but Rufus, Brian, and I played every day
after lunch. We expanded to five-card draw,
seven-card stud, dealer's choice, even deuces wild.
Brian and Rufus learned the words: straight,
flush, four of a kind, ante, and raise.

Brian loved the game (better than Concentration) and played enthusiastically. At first he
cheerfully named all the cards in his hand out
loud, talking to the nice queens, telling them he'd
find another. But he soon learned to play without
a word, silently, competently, remembering everything, showing no trace of emotion, winning con-
sistently, his pile of chips three times as high as
Rufus's and mine.

I figured he was ready. When I was dealer I
stacked my hand with aces, dealt off the bottom,
slipped cards from the middle. Brian's pile of
chips dwindled; mine rose. Rufus's pile was as

small as ever, but he continued to play with dogged determination.

This was taking too long. When was Brian going to catch on? I blatantly slid an ace into my hand to replace another card and Rufus yelled, "Hey, Mary, you can't do that!"

"Do what?" I arranged my hand.

"You took another card. I saw you."

I looked at Rufus coolly. "Who says so?"

"I do!" yelled Rufus. "Didn't she, Brian? Didn't she steal another card?"

Brian's hands began to flap. "Doesn't matter. Nice queens. Doesn't matter, Rufus. Let's just play."

We played and my aces won easily over Brian's queens.

I pulled in the chips and dealt another hand, "Deuces wild," I said, spotting a two of spades that I could sneak from the deck.

"She did it again!" Rufus yelled. "Brian, you had to see her that time."

Brian lowered his head. "Doesn't matter. Just play."

I put down the cards. "It does matter, Bri. It matters a lot. That's called cheating, and any time you see it happen get out of the game. Don't yell, that's no good, Ruf. But don't 'just play' either."

Brian was very sad. "I like to play. Why do I have to get out of the game? Doesn't matter if I win."

Sometimes it seemed to me that the kids I

taught, or was supposed to be teaching, saw the
world more clearly than anyone else. Sometimes I
thought if they could all just live together somewhere they would have a kind of Utopia, where
there were lots of presents, but it didn't matter
who gave or got, and lots of games, but it wasn't
important who won or lost.

Brian had known all along that I was cheating,
but what did he care? If he didn't care about
winning. I could make a fool of myself all day
long while he still got what he wanted: the fun of
playing.

"Okay, Bri," I said. "Never mind. Let's forget
this poker-playing lesson. Just do me a favor, all
right? If you're playing for money next year—real
money, not chips—and you see somebody cheating, fold up your cards when it's your turn to bet,
like you do when you have a bad hand, and pass.
All right?"

Brian looked at me quizzically, "Yeah, sure,
Mary. Nobody'd want to lose real money."

He probably would have known what to do all
along, but I kept on, trying to anticipate, to alert
him to the ways of the city.

"Do you know what drugs are?" I asked him
one day.

"Yes. Anacin, Bayer Aspirin, Bufferin—'stops
acidity while it stops the pain.' I saw it—"

"Yeah, Bri. Okay, I know. You saw it on television." How to even begin to tell him about
marijuana, grass, pot, dope, amphetamines, speed,

cocaine, uppers, downers? Maybe television was as good a way as any. "Try to keep it that way," I said. "If you've seen the drug advertised on TV, it's okay to use. If you haven't, don't touch it."

I shook my head at myself. I, who had decried commercials, claiming they whetted appetites with false promises, now was advocating them. You never know.

On the subject of money: "Take as little to school as possible. Just enough for lunch. And if you can, get lunch tickets instead."

Sex. We'd been over masturbation many times. It was a large part of our reality, and on this, at least, we were probably more savvy than P.S. 24. The code here was—do it when you're alone. Not in public. I didn't attempt the topic of intercourse, homosexuality, sodomy, rape. Brian would probably be exposed to all of these and more, but somehow it seemed too much for our crash course. I'd answer whatever questions came up and make sure he knew how to find Bernie Sorrino.

Weapons. Don't fight back if somebody has a knife, a gun, a razor blade, a broken bottle. They're not thinking straight. Keep quiet and give them whatever you can. Try not to walk alone.

Alone. That was going to be the hardest thing. Brian would be alone. Most of our kids were always alone outside of school. It was not that they were true loners; they would have loved to play with the neighborhood kids, but no matter how they improved they were still a little "different," and the neighborhood kids, in good, all-American style, shunned what was different.

It was time to go down to the school now, to P.S. 24. I'd given out my tiny store of advice. I'd cheated and demanded that Brian catch me at it. I'd served him helpings that were too small, gypped him out of his turn, and made him insist on his rights. I had conned him, deceived him, challenged him—and he'd survived. Now I'd better go and see the school itself.

The March winds whipped scraps of trash and newspaper across the streets as I drove in early in the morning. The city was bigger than I had imagined it, most of it old, some of it beautiful. Delicately proportioned church spires rose unexpectedly beside dirty tenements and tacky department stores.

The junior high school was on the far side of the business district in a flat, open area, opposite an empty warehouse. I parked my car in the warehouse lot and picked my way across the street over beer cans and broken bottles. The school looked as if it had been decorated for a holiday with bright cloth at every window. But as I approached I realized that this was no decoration, these were live kids hanging out of the windows, whistling and hooting, analyzing each inch of my anatomy and commenting on every step I took. I looked up, waved at them, and the hoots died down a little. Suddenly a long, loud, insistent bell rang and immediately the bodies withdrew, windows slammed shut, and there was absolute silence as I walked up the chipped concrete steps.

There was a sign by the front door: VISITORS MUST REPORT DIRECTLY TO THE OFFICE. PASSES ARE REQUIRED FOR ENTRANCE.

Depression crept around my heart and curdled in my stomach. This was a school? It seemed more like a prison.

In the office a dry, acid-looking woman refused to speak to me, pointing to a pad and paper. I filled out the form. She read it reluctantly, checked by phone, and issued me a pass for Room 342.

There were guards at the head and foot of each stairway. The halls were windowless and the doors to the rooms were tightly shut. Boy, I thought, you got a long way to go yourself, Bernie.

This was unfair. I couldn't hold Bernie Sorrino accountable for the whole city school system; his job was special education. The class I had come to visit was labeled SGI, a term I had never heard before. It translated to Special Grade Instruction.

"What it means is," Bernie had told me, "that these kids don't fit anyplace else. But they don't fit together either, so there's no name for 'em. Can't put 'em in a retarded class, can't put 'em in a regular transient class, going from room to room for different subjects, so we put 'em together, teach 'em everything in one room, and hope they survive. What's the matter, sweetheart? You don't like it? It's one helluva lot better than anything else we got to offer."

Bernie's words went round in my head as I hesitated outside Room 342 while the stairway guard eyed me suspiciously. I couldn't retreat now. I took a deep breath and pulled open the heavy door, prepared for the worst. I couldn't have been more surprised.

The room was filled with sunshine and perhaps a dozen kids. Some desks were pushed together, others not. The kids were all crowded in the back of the room in front of a makeshift grocery store. They barely glanced at me, busily making out orders, consulting shopping lists, compiling items, wrapping, paying, giving, getting money.

A young woman with a wide smile and round glasses sat on the back windowsill refereeing. "Come on in. You must be Mary MacCracken. Bernie told me you were coming. I'm Katie Moresco. Think you can stand the noise?"

I could have stood anything, I felt so good about having her in the room. I stayed all morning, impressed by the way she handled the kids, by her warmth and her competence. The books and teaching materials were worn and shabby, but at least this meant they were used, and there was a lot more variety than we had. The kids themselves were twelve to fourteen years old;

about half were black. Some of their young faces reflected anger and almost a bone weariness; their clothes were torn and their hands grimy, but there was no look of retardation—and on that morning, anyway, no bizarre acting out.

At lunchtime the kids lined up at the door and then filed out to the lunchroom.

I turned to Katie Moresco. "Brian's lucky. This will be good for him."

She barely heard me. "The mortality rate is high in that lunchroom. Good thing you came in the morning; in the afternoon we have the walking wounded. Somebody always comes back bleeding: bloody nose, cut lip, broken arm. And you know whose fault they say it is? My kids!

"They blame everything on the 'specials'—not just the kids, the teachers too. Sometimes I could kill them, I really could. If they're not blaming it on my kids, they're looking the other way while the rest of the school beats up on them. Last year I got so mad I ate with them every day down there. This year I figure they got to learn to live in a jungle sometime."

She took her own sandwich from her desk drawer. "Come on down to the teachers' room and have a cup of coffee with your lunch."

I hadn't brought lunch, hadn't even thought about it, I was so used to eating franks and beans with the kids. But I liked Katie Moresco and wanted to keep talking. "Can I buy you a hamburger?"

Katie dropped her sandwich in the wastebasket without hesitation. "Fantastic. Let's go."

Relish, mustard, ketchup, Katie poured them all on top of her hamburger and grinned at me over the bun. "Thanks. That school has all the charm of the Tombs. I love the kids, but the rest of the place gives me the creeps," she said. "Listen, what's this Brian like? Think he'll fit in okay?"

I described our school and Brian as thoroughly as I could. Katie listened carefully, interrupting from time to time to ask a question or explore a point more explicitly.

"Well," she said finally. "From what you say, it should work out. Sounds like he's about on the same reading level as Joe; math he can do with Trixie; socially—well, we'll just have to see."

I dropped Katie back at school when we'd finished lunch. "Thanks again. I'll bring Brian down to visit in another few weeks, if that's all right with you. You'll be back next fall?" I wanted the assurance, realizing how important she would be in a successful transition for Brian.

Katie ducked her head so she could look in the car window. "Yeah. Sure. Unless I get lucky and start growing a kid. But don't hold your breath. I've been trying to get pregnant five years steady, so it's not likely to happen this summer. See you."

She straightened, hesitated, then bent back down.

"Listen, about this social thing. I mean about Brian's getting along with the other kids. I was

thinking maybe I could arrange something. . . .
Where does he live, which section? I mean, which
bus will he be riding?"

Her question felt like a clout. Bus? I forced my
voice out. "Pine Street. One-eighty-seven Pine. I
don't know, I'm not sure about the section."

The school bell jangled and Katie backed up
waving as I stepped on the accelerator. I had to
get back.

Brian. My God, of course, he'd be riding buses.
No more the isolated splendor of the taxi. Brian
would have to learn to ride a bus.

The next day the four kids and I sat in the
small three-sided bus shelter in the middle of our
town. We took up the rear bench and the children
sat silently, looking at the wide expanse of grass
and trees in the park across from us. I knew
they'd much rather be over there, away from the
curious, sometimes hostile eyes that stared at us.
For that matter, so would I.

"Now look," I said, as quietly as I could.
"There's nothing to this. We've been all over it at
school. We've drawn it on the blackboard and
talked about it. We get on here, take the bus to
Glendale, get off, walk around the town, take the
bus back.

"I'm going to pay for Hannah, Jamie, Rufus,
and myself. Brian, you've got your money; you'll
buy your own ticket."

Brian nodded and the silence continued. Rufus

was the only one who'd ever been on a bus. That was over a year ago and his sister had been carsick.

I looked at my watch. The bus was five minutes late and the station was beginning to get crowded. The tension got to Jamie and he stood up in front of the bench and planted one foot before the other and began to rock back and forth. A dozen pairs of adult eyes stared at him. I stood up, not so much to block his rocking as to give him some protection from the curious stares.

But as the bus pulled in the people forgot Jamie and rushed outside, trying to be first on line, although the bus was almost empty. I shepherded Rufus, Hannah, and Jamie in front of me—Brian was so close behind that he stepped on me twice. I paid our fares and moved down the aisle; Brian panicked and kept following.

"Here, Mary, you pay, you pay." He thrust the quarter into my hand.

The driver yelled, "Get back here, sonny. I saw you sneak by."

I turned Brian around and walked back with him, thankful at least that I'd given him the exact fare.

"Give the man the money, Bri."

Gingerly Brian dropped the quarter into the driver's outstretched hand, careful not to let his fingers touch.

The driver glared at me. "What's the matter, lady? Can't you handle your·kids? They get worse every year. You gotta watch 'em all the time, otherwise they steal you blind."

There wasn't time to answer. Jamie was rocking up and down the aisle. Hannah had twisted her cropped hair into little clumps as she waited for the bus, and now she pulled at them and moaned as she knelt on one of the seats, head buried against the cushion. Rufus sat loyally, miserably, beside her.

I ushered Brian and Jamie in front of me, gathered up Rufus and Hannah on the way, and finally got us all seated. Two women moved away and we sat like pariahs in the rear of the bus.

The ride itself was uneventful but joyless. Even the walk down Glendale's streets was glum. Ordinarily, the children loved to window-shop, but now they stared blankly at the displays. There wasn't any point in buying the ice cream cones I'd planned.

We walked down one side of the main street, back the other, and took the next bus back. It had taken the whole afternoon, that one miserable bus ride. In some ways it didn't really seem worth it.

But we rode the bus twice the next week. Things were getting better. The driver and some of the passengers began to recognize us—and sometimes even smile.

The next week I gave Brian a dollar. When he waited for his change, the driver said, "Atta boy. Better count it. Make sure I didn't cheat you. Ha-ha."

Brian, of course, counted the change right then and there: fifty, seventy-five, eighty-five, ninety, one dollar. Both the driver and the passengers behind him waited patiently while he did it.

The first sunny day in April I put Brian on the bus alone. We all drove to the station, we all waited for the bus, but only Brian would ride.

My heart sank when the bus pulled in and I saw an unfamiliar driver.

"I don't want to go, Mary," Brian said. "Not today. Maybe tomorrow."

"Hurry up," I said. "There's not much time."

Brian paid his quarter and sat down next to the window, pressing his sad, pointed face as close to us as he could. Rufus, Hannah, and Jamie all waved cheerfully, they were so glad not to be there themselves.

As soon as the bus left, I got the other three children into the car and drove to Glendale, hurrying so we'd be there when the bus drove in. We arrived in plenty of time to see Brian get off with tears running down his cheeks.

"What's the matter, Brian?"

"She was scary. That lady next to me was mean and scary—and she had a black umbrella. It isn't even raining. That could have been a broom. A folded-up broom."

"That's ridiculous, Brian. If she's scary, ignore her or move. You're doing fine."

And the next day I put him back on the bus.

At night, before I slept, his pale, worried face peered at me from the window of the bus, and I'd think, I want him back, riding in the car with us, safe and happy. But the next day I'd drive him to the bus station and pick him up at the other end. At least we were getting speedier; if we ate lunch fast, we could get down and back with almost no study time lost.

The next week Rufus wanted to ride with Brian. Why not? Brian even paid Rufus's fare. They sat together, smiling, as the bus pulled out.

The following week Hannah wanted to go too. I was less sure about this. Rufus was hardly a sophisticate, but he had ten times more social know-how than Hannah did. But Brian was enthusiastic, and after all, that was what the whole thing was about, getting Brian to like bus riding. I finally agreed and the two boys and Hannah planned their trip carefully, setting it up for the coming Friday.

This time we really would celebrate. We wouldn't just have cones. We'd sit down in the store and have real ice cream sodas.

All three dressed up that Friday. Brian wore his blue plaid shirt and sweater, Rufus had on his oxford-cloth button-down shirt, and Hannah wore her sailor dress and shiny black shoes and carried a large black purse, just like her mother's. Evidently traveling meant pocketbooks in the Rosnic household.

Jamie and I watched them board and find seats

together in the back and then we went back to the car, feeling a little lonesome. "Never mind, Jamie, we'll go out by the dump and you can drive the car, okay?"

The dump was actually a deserted marsh with an unpaved road running around the edge. When we got there I lifted Jamie onto my lap and let him hold the wheel and honk the horn while we drove twice around.

The bus arrived at the Glendale stop just as we did. Obviously, something was wrong. The driver turned off the motor, put on his red blinkers, and climbed down out of the bus. Hannah, Brian, and Rufus followed. Hannah's face was tear-stained; Brian was hopping around, hands flapping against his sides; Rufus was grinning.

The bus driver was our familiar one, and he came up to me without ado. "Well, missus, you can be real proud of this young fella here," he pointed at Brian. "Captured a criminal, that's what."

"A criminal?" I said. Maybe I was getting a little punchy myself.

"Yes, ma'am, a thief. We got him on the bus now, got two fellas watching him for me. Would've taken him straight to the police station, but I knew you'd be waiting and I didn't want you worried. But we're going there right now, turn him over to the law."

The story was taking too long for Rufus. "He got Hannah's purse—"

"That's right," the driver continued. "These here children of yours were just sitting there, riding like regular ladies and gentlemen. Then I pulled in to make my first stop back there on South Road. You know the spot?"

"That's when he grabbed Hannah's purse!" shouted Rufus. "And then Brian—"

"Yup. Then this young fella"—the driver's big hand came down on Brian's shoulder—"was up like a streak and down the aisle ahead of the hoodlum. Blocked him right off there by my station until—"

"And Brian shoved too, Mary, and he yelled," Rufus went on. "Brian yelled at the guy, 'Give it back,' and then the guy tried to get by Brian, but Brian didn't let him. I mean he really gave it to that guy. Brian stuck out his foot and tripped him and the guy fell down and the driver got up and grabbed him."

Hannah smiled around her tears, holding up the black pocketbook. "Driver hold him and then Bri-an grab my purse. Get it back for me. Had real money."

When I looked at the cold facts I could see that all that Brian had actually done was to chase the purse-snatcher down the aisle, trip him, and then reclaim Hannah's purse after the bus driver had pinned the thief. Still, this would have been an achievement for any twelve-year-old boy, and for Brian it was a four-star event. The marvelous thing was that the other kids knew it. They built

Brian up, exaggerated his courage, and, most of all, recognized what it had meant to him.

Brian stood quietly now, his hands in his pockets. He didn't say anything. He didn't have to. He had the confidence of a hero.

18

On Saturday morning, along with the bills, a letter arrived from the Board. I propped it against the bowl of daffodils and studied it while I drank my orange juice. I was getting less and less eager to read these missives from the Board.

I finally opened it with my second cup of coffee. It was typed, impersonal, addressed to "All members of the staff," signed by Jean Huntington, Board President.

The letter was only two paragraphs long. The first paragraph asked each teaching member of the staff to send two photostatic copies of his teaching certificate and undergraduate and master degrees. The second paragraph stated that it was necessary to file one copy with the state; the Board would keep the other. Jean Huntington thanked each of us for our cooperation.

I had no degree, undergraduate or otherwise, and no teaching certificate. I did have a list of the credits I'd gotten during my two years at Wellesley years before, and another list of the journalism and psychology courses I'd taken later, although not for credit. And I had my twelve education credits. I typed these up carefully and mailed them to the Board.

A week later I received a two-paragraph letter stating that they found it "regrettable" but my present credentials were "inadequate." The final paragraph asked me to advise them of my plans.

What plans? The phrase seemed ominous, and again I took the letter to the Director.

She read it quickly. The thought crossed my mind that of course she must have seen it before. It was sent from the Board, and she was on the Board.

"What should I do?" I asked. She had hired me, taught me, had me train other teachers. She had been in the field over fourteen years. I was certain she'd know how to handle it.

She lit a cigarette and studied me over the smoke. "There doesn't seem to be an awful lot you can do, Mary. This state aid is going to be a godsend, but I'm afraid it's going to mean we're going to lose some of our best teachers."

Lose. What was she talking about? I had no intention of being lost. I was a teacher, an experienced, qualified teacher. She knew it. I knew it. I intended to keep on teaching; the only question was how.

"Now, look," I said. "What I'm trying to say, to find out, is how to get the papers that will satisfy the Board. I'm taking the courses as fast as I can, but I need some sort of dispensation or whatever, until I get my degree."

The Director stood up, obviously dismissing me.

"Well, good luck," she said. "I hope it works out for you." Vaguely she waved the cigarette as she picked up the phone.

I got the message, finally. The Director wasn't going to help. She might like me, might think I was a good teacher, but she wasn't about to stick her neck out. Her dream, her "impossible dream" of her own school, was too close. She wouldn't risk fouling it up for one teacher. Good teachers came and went during the lifetime of a woman like the Director, but there was only one school. I didn't blame her. The school was her life. She had put all her strength, all her money, all her energy into keeping that school alive over the years. Now it— and she—were almost safe. My problems must seem very small.

"How'd it go?" Patty asked as I came in late for Circle.

I shook my head. "Not so good. I'll have to think of something else. Maybe I'll go see Bernie Sorrino after school."

It was hot in Bernie's office and he had an electric fan going.

"Sit down," he said. "What's June gonna be like if it's hot as hell in May? What can I do for you, sweetheart?"

I showed him the correspondence from the Board. He studied it carefully and then handed it back.

"What's the old lady say, that Director of yours?"

"She wishes me good luck."

"Yeah. Well, that figures. You're going to need more than luck, I'm afraid. If she was willing to stick her neck out and cover for you, you might get away with it. It's still a private school and they got a lot more leeway than we do. I'd hire you in a minute if I could, you know that. Still with that new school and state support, she's gonna be looked at pretty close. Probably doesn't want to take the chance."

"Listen, Bernie. This doesn't make any sense. I'm taking the courses, not learning much, but taking the courses and getting A's. I've been in our school six years altogether—teaching full time with salary for five. I like it; I want to keep on teaching. The state must want experienced teachers who want to teach. Am I wrong?"

"That's right, you're wrong. The state doesn't give a damn, unless it looks good on paper."

Frustration was mounting inside me. "Okay, then. I'll get the paper. Where do I go? What do I do?"

Bernie wiped his forehead. "You can't get a paper. Not without a degree of some kind. If you had a degree in paperhanging, even, you might get provisional certification while you finish your education courses. Without it you haven't got a chance."

I stood up. "Thank you, Bern. I appreciate your taking time to talk to me. I know how busy you are. But you're wrong about one thing. There's always a chance."

Bernie stood up with me, shaking his head, lighting a cigar at the same time. "Don't break your heart, sweetheart. It's not worth it. You remind me of that filly at the racetrack, headlong, smart, but you're gonna run smack into the wall if you don't watch out. Listen, why don't you get married?"

I stopped by the office door. "Proposing?"

"Jesus," he said. "Bigamy. That's what you're trying to involve me in. Ruin my saintly reputation. Listen now," he said, his face serious. "Keep me informed. Let me know what happens."

"Yes," I said. "I will. Thanks again."

19

"Open your mouth, babe. Let me take a look."
Hannah obediently opened her mouth wide and I
peered inside. Her front teeth looked deceptively
good, but the back and side teeth were discolored
and broken or rotten.

"Does that hurt?"

Hannah shook her head, talking around my finger. "Uh-uh." Then, forcing my finger out with
her tongue, she said, "I no go dentist doctor."

"Boy, that's about the silliest thing you've ever
said. Your teeth need to be fixed and the dentist
can fix them."

Hannah shook her head at me again. "Dentist
doctor bad. Hurt Carl. No let Mama sit chair with
me. Bite dentist doctor. Hate him."

"For Pete's sake, what kind of sense does that
make? How can the dentist fix your teeth if your
mother's in the chair? How can he fix anything if
you bite him?" I shook my own head at her.

Mrs. Rosnic had called the school and left word
that it was urgent that I call her back as soon as
possible. When I did she explained that Hannah

refused to go to the dentist and wanted me to look at Hannah's teeth.

Mrs. Rosnic was right. It was urgent. I had never seen such bad teeth. I sighed, wishing I'd looked before, wishing again that we had some sort of school doctor, or at least someone to do occasional routine checkups.

There was always so much to be done, never enough time to do it. I shook my head, feeling a little weary but knowing part of my weariness was because my reply to the Board was still hanging fire. More than a week now and I still hadn't come up with anything. Well, anyway, what counted now were Hannah's teeth, and I called Mrs. Rosnic after school to tell her I agreed that Hannah should see a dentist immediately.

It turned out that what Mrs. Rosnic actually wanted was for me to find a new dentist for her. Hannah hadn't been kidding; she had bitten the other man and he refused to see her again. I promised to discuss it with the Director and see what I could find out.

There was a formality between the Director and myself that hadn't been there previously. It was almost as though she feared I would reopen the subject of the letter from the Board of Directors and was purposely insulating herself from discussion with me. She never spoke to me now without a cigarette in her hand, the smoke forming another screen between us.

However, she was always courteous, and now

she suggested I call the mother of a child who had just undergone extensive dental work. I thanked her and then sat without saying anything for a minute or two, watching the thin gray smoke curl before my eyes. I thought she might want to talk, but she, too, sat silently and then turned to the phone, excusing herself.

Both the child's teacher and the mother highly recommended Dr. Sullivan, a dentist who specialized in treating children. I reported back to Mrs. Rosnic and the Director and then called Dr. Sullivan.

His schedule was crowded, his secretary said, but there was a cancellation for Thursday, May 14, at ten thirty.

I made the appointment for Hannah and called Mrs. Rosnic, but then it turned out that she hadn't realized it was so far and she didn't like to drive on highways and she didn't see how she could leave Grandpa and Helen, and—well, really what she was hoping was that I'd take Hannah.

More conferences with the Director, arrangements for the boys to join other classes while I was gone. Finally everything was set. And then on May 14 Hannah didn't come to school!

I called the Rosnics' house and Mrs. Rosnic said she was sorry but Hannah was up to her old tricks again—wouldn't get on the bus, wouldn't come to school.

It was nine forty-five. There was no way we could make the ten-thirty appointment. All those arrangements for nothing, Dr. Sullivan's time wasted—just because Hannah had managed to have her own way.

"Mrs. Rosnic," I said. "I'll call Dr. Sullivan and apologize—and somehow or other get another appointment. Tell Hannah that, and tell her that we're going to keep this one."

"Maybe if we don't tell her ... ?" Mrs. Rosnic suggested hopefully.

"We'll tell her. She trusts us and it's no fair taking advantage. Tell her I'll see her in school tomorrow morning."

Hannah dragged into school the next morning, glared at me, and went into the coat closet. I ignored her and after a while she couldn't stand it any longer and came out.

"Not going to dentist doctor," she stated unequivocally.

"That's right, lovey. Not today. Next week."

"You mean! Hate you! Why I have to go? You not go!"

"I'm going," I said. "I'm going with you. Besides, I go see my own dentist twice a year."

"Two times every year?"

"Mm-hmm. He cleans my teeth and fixes anything that needs fixing."

Hannah came over close to me, staring hard at my mouth. Then she put out her hand and I opened my mouth while she explored my teeth with her finger.

"What call that?" she asked, running her finger over the top of my lower teeth.

"Teeth."

"No. Not teeth. Inside teeth."

"Silver. Silver fillings."

"Silver," she repeated. "All white and silver. Is nice."

"Thank you."

"Two times every year?"

"Mm-hmm."

"That lot of times. You go hundred times already."

"Hey, come on. I'm not that old."

Hannah removed her finger from my mouth. "You sit in chair, okay? I sit on you."

"Nope. The dentist, his name is Dr. Sullivan, can't fix your teeth that way. But I'll be with you. We'll drive down together in the car and go into the office together. The dentist has two rooms, at least my dentist does, and you'll be in one room and I'll be in the other. It will probably take about a half hour, and then we'll drive back together."

"Maybe I not come. Maybe stay home."

"We stood Dr. Sullivan up once. We're not going to do it again. This time our appointment is for eleven. If you don't show up at school, I'll be over to pick you up at home."

The morning of the fourteenth was sunny and hot and Hannah sat close beside me in the car, her arm pressed against my side. I knew she was scared and I didn't blame her, but she rode quietly, looking straight ahead.

We found Dr. Sullivan's office on a quiet side street and Hannah sat beside the secretary's desk and gave the required information by herself, spelling her last name carefully, giving her address, phone number, even her birth date.

For another child this would be good, showing composure and intelligence; for Hannah it was spectacular. Nine months ago she had lain on the floor howling and screaming. Now, immediately before going in to see the dentist, she could sit and quietly give her personal data.

Dr. Sullivan came into the waiting room and greeted us in a slow, kind voice and then invited us both into the examining room. He was a slight man, with a thin face, thin hair, and tired eyes that peered out from behind his glasses. I was surprised to be asked into the examining room, but I followed along and waited in the doorway.

His touch was sure and skillful as he helped Hannah into the dental chair, gave her a ride up and down, and asked if he could look into her mouth. There was something special about the way he asked: a gentleness, a courtesy. I was pleased and touched by the respect with which this small thin man treated Hannah.

After a few minutes he came over to the doorway where I stood. "We'll need X rays. But even without them I can tell you there's going to be a lot of work. It will be extremely painful; we'll have to pull at least two teeth and maybe more. She'll need anesthesia."

"Is there any alternative?" I asked. "She's had some bad experiences before, and though she seems calm, it's taking a lot of effort. She's very frightened."

"The work has to be done, even on the baby teeth. Otherwise it will just get worse and the infections will drain into her whole system. Will she take gas? How about finances? Can the family afford it?"

"I think Hannah will be all right, especially if you continue as you did today. And the finances we can work out. Does the money have to be paid all at once?"

"No, of course not. Let me take the X rays and then I can tell you how much it will run. Why don't you go on out to the waiting room now?"

I walked over to where Hannah sat. She seemed so tiny in contrast to the big chair, and her courage was even more apparent. I told her I'd be in the waiting room and that there would be no hurt today, only pictures to see what needed to be done.

In fifteen minutes Hannah and Dr. Sullivan were back. While Hannah picked out a gold ring set with an imitation ruby from a velvet tray, Dr. Sullivan spoke quietly to me. "I couldn't have asked for a better patient. I'll start with the teeth that can be saved, get those filled so they won't get worse. But I'm still going to have to pull two." Anger tinged his voice. "Why didn't you bring her in earlier?"

I knew how he felt. I often felt this way at school. Why had it been so long? It would have been so much easier earlier.

"I just got her this year."

"Okay. Okay. She should have been in years ago. Sorry. Didn't mean to jump on you."

"I know," I said. "How much will it run?"

"Family pretty hard up?"

"Very."

"Let's keep it to a hundred dollars. Is that all right?"

"That's fine. Now, what's going to happen next time? I think it will be easier if she knows what to expect."

Dr. Sullivan took off his glasses and rubbed his eyes. "You know, you're only the second person who's ever asked me that. Usually they leave it all up to me."

Anger flashed in his eyes for a short minute. "Maybe I'm judging too harshly, but I can't help noticing that parents seem to have abdicated. They just bring the child; that's all they seem to figure is required of them. Get the child here on any excuse, lie to him, often as not—then they wonder why kids don't trust dentists."

He sighed, the anger gone, and put his glasses back on carefully, almost delicately, tucking the wire sidepieces behind his ears. "Hard to know the best way to approach a child like Hannah. I think I'll use gas even for the fillings. I could use novocaine, but that big needle's pretty scary for

any kid and she's probably had more than her
share of fright. Tell her ... wait. Come on back in
for a minute. I'll show her; that's better than trying to tell her."

The waiting room was filled now with mothers
and children, two of whom were crying. Hannah
sat on a leather chair, hands in her lap, examining
her new ring, and I felt another surge of pride in
her composure.

"Hannah, we're all through for today. Dr. Sullivan says you were a great patient, one of the
best he's ever had. If you want to, we can go back
in for a minute and see something he wants to
show you, so you'll know what's going to happen
next time."

Hannah slid off the leather chair and put her
hand in mine and I could feel the new ring sliding on her finger. Back in the examining room, we
both looked at the mask that Dr. Sullivan held in
his hands.

"Sleep stuff?" Hannah asked. Was it possible
memories of that infant operation were stirring in
her head?

"Not really sleep. Dreams. Do you ever dream?"

Hannah nodded. "All time. Dream mouses.
Dream Blue Fairy. Dream all time."

Dr. Sullivan put the mask over his own head.
He looked ridiculous because he had left on his
glasses and now he peered at us with an odd
wall-eyed look. But I wanted to put my arms
around him. He cared more about Hannah than

himself, or how he looked. Who would ever expect to find a true lover in the dentist's office?

"Now you figure out the best dream you can have, Hannah, and next week, while I'm fixing your teeth, we'll see if we can find it for you."

All the way home in the car, Hannah turned the ruby ring against her finger. Finally she said, "He nice, that dentist doctor. Not bite him."

The next two visits were harder, but each time when Hannah and Dr. Sullivan returned to where I sat in the waiting room he had his arm around her.

Finally he said to me, "Well, that's it for repair. Next time I'll pull those two teeth." He lowered his voice. "It may be a little rough. One of those teeth is so far gone, I'm going to have trouble getting a grip on it. I'll do my best."

I nodded. If Hannah had to go through this I was glad she was in kind, competent hands.

"I talked to Mrs. Rosnic about the money," I said. "Will it be all right if she sends you two dollars a week?"

He hesitated and I said quickly, "If you'd rather, I can give you a check now and she can send the money to the school."

His voice was hot. "Don't be foolish. It's not that. It's just . . . having to mail two dollars every week. Life's so hard for some people. Seems like there ought to be an easier way to live."

Hannah had been in the dental room for forty-seven minutes. I had turned endless pages of magazines and now I walked to the window of the crowded office, hardly hearing the noises of the other children and their mothers. It shouldn't be taking so long—two teeth! How long can you pull on a tooth?

Dr. Sullivan put his hand on the middle of my back and I turned, startled, from the window.

"She's all right," he said immediately. "But still groggy. I had to give her a pretty heavy dose of anesthetic, but I finally got everything out. Here."

He handed me a bottle filled with clear liquid and two teeth, or rather one tooth and pieces of another.

"Have her rinse her mouth every couple of hours with warm salt water. If she's in a lot of pain, grind up one of these tablets and mix it with a little sugar and water. Call me if there's any trouble; otherwise I'll see her once more, just to check everything out. Come on in now."

We walked together into the examining room and over to the big dental chair where Hannah lay, her eyes still closed.

"I'm sorry about her dress," Dr. Sullivan said, touching the splotches of dark red blood.

At his touch Hannah opened her eyes.

"Hannah," he said, "you were very brave. It's all over now and I won't do this to you again. Do you want to get a new ring?"

Hannah shook her head. One was enough for

her. She wore her ruby ring each day, her finger turning steadily greener underneath it.

"I have her mouth packed so she isn't able to speak much. Take it out in about an hour and let her rinse."

I put out my hand to Hannah and she took it and followed me to the door. Then I turned back and put out my other hand to Dr. Sullivan.

"Thank you."

"Yes. Well, be sure you bring her regularly now." He touched Hannah's shoulder. "You really were a good girl. The best girl ever."

Hannah dozed beside me all the way back, her head on my shoulder. I drove as carefully as I could, while in my head the words went round: "The best girl, the best girl, the best girl ever...."

We were almost back to school when I changed my mind. I turned the car around and, with Hannah still asleep, I drove to my apartment.

She followed me groggily out of the car and leaned against me as I unlocked the apartment door. Up the yellow-carpeted stairs to the couch in the living room. I sat down and put my feet up on the coffee table and Hannah cuddled down beside me.

My heart was pounding. I knew I shouldn't be doing this. The school and Mrs. Rosnic both thought we were at the dentist's. I had no permission to bring Hannah to my home. But I wanted her there so badly. I wanted just to keep her a little longer, keep her safe.

Hannah opened her eyes briefly and stared around the room. "Is nice," she said.

I slipped off her dress, washed out the stains in cold water and hung the dress on the back porch to dry. Then I sat down again beside Hannah while she slept. I waited till her sleep was deep enough so that I could move without disturbing her, and then I got up and went to my writing desk.

I had to try again. I couldn't leave Hannah. Not yet. She was still too vulnerable, still on the verge of becoming. There was still too much to do.

Dear Mrs. Huntington,

I am writing to ask if you and the Board of Directors will reconsider your decision of last week. I know that on paper my credits are lacking, but I'm sure if I could talk to you and the Board about my position, I could explain . . .

When I had finished the letter I woke Hannah, led her to the bathroom, and took out the cotton packing as gently as I could. She rinsed her mouth, put her dress on, and then, feeling better, ate a dish of raspberry sherbet.

All the way back to school she held the small glass vial of teeth. When we arrived she removed Henry's flowers from my table and set the little bottle there instead.

"Keep tooths there," she said as the boys watched in awe.

I kept them there for the rest of the year and I have them still, wrapped in tissue in a small white box inside my bureau drawer.

20

Jean Huntington called me during lunchtime at the school.

"I'm speaking officially, Mary, as Board President. I'm only the spokesman for the Board. I hope you understand that. It's not going to be possible for you to appear at a Board meeting. I'm sorry, but it's against all previous precedent. There is an appointed spokesman for teachers, your Director. She is the official member of the Board who represents all teachers. Whatever business you have should be presented through her."

"I see. All right."

"Mary. Please wait a minute. Speaking now as a friend, not Board President, whatever I can do—well, I know how much the school means to you."

"Thank you, Jean. I'll write something up and give it to the Director. When's the Board meeting?"

"Actually—uh, tomorrow night. Things are just incredibly busy. . . . You wouldn't believe—"

"I know," I said, remembering the phrases. "This time of year . . ."

"Exactly. Well, I knew you'd understand. And I will do whatever—"

"Right. Thanks again."

The floor by the telephone in the Director's office seemed like quicksand, and I felt as if I were sinking, going under. I replaced the phone and hurried back to my classroom.

If Jean's days were hectic, ours were chaotic. We were in the midst of a crisis and there was no time to think about anything except the immediate moment.

One of the younger children had come down with measles. Her teacher was three months' pregnant and decided the risk of exposure was too great so she was out and the Director had taken over her class.

Yesterday two more mothers called reporting measles. Worse than that, Patty had caught the measles too and was very ill. I talked to Ted on the phone each night. He was staying home, but the doctor thought they might have to move Patty to the hospital.

With Patty out, her class became bedlam. Tina undressed not only on the bus but all day long. Wanda Gomez bit her arm and slapped her face. At lunch Barbara Lasky massaged franks and beans into her hair as if they were shampoo, and Janie laughed hysterically all day and then gouged a hunk out of the Director's arm on her way to the bus.

In one way, it underlined Patty's excellence. When she was there her room was quiet and peaceful. The girls studied, read, worked diligently in their workbooks; in the afternoon they did various arts and crafts projects. Patty had taught both Wanda and Tina to knit, and I loved to walk into their room and find Patty and the girls sitting around a table like a Wednesday ladies' sewing circle. But without Patty the room fell apart. The girls could not sustain what she had taught them; their security was based in Patty and they seemed able to function only in the atmosphere that she provided.

There was no crisis teacher in our school, though other schools like ours use one at times like this. A crisis teacher is a regular part of the school but doesn't have a class of her own. Instead she goes wherever she is needed, coping with the most difficult problems, taking over in emergencies.

If we had had such a teacher, perhaps she could have handled Patty's class during the measles epidemic with a minimum of disruption. As it was, we all rocked in chaos during the day and dropped into bed exhausted at night.

The Director hired one substitute after another to handle Patty's class during the morning hours; not one lasted more than a day. We struggled through lunch alone, the eight children and myself. In the afternoon, the Director divided the girls up, parceling them out to different classrooms.

My children, because they were closer to Patty's class, joining them for Circle and for lunch, were more affected by Patty's absence than the rest of the school. I tried to be kinder, stronger, more patient, knowing how difficult it was for them. But I was in a turmoil as well. I couldn't help but wonder if my presence was as crucial to my children as Patty's was to her class. If so, what would happen next year if the worst should occur and I couldn't come back?

I began to look at my four even more closely. Brian was going to be all right, I was sure of that. Ever since he had rescued Hannah's purse on the bus ride, he had grown steadier, bolder, more competent. He would be going to P.S. 24 in the fall and he was going to make it. He had dealt with the outside world now, and just the dealing with it had reduced his terror.

Rufus was almost ready. Square, solid, loving Rufus, his plumpness almost gone, never absent any more. No pseudo-illnesses, no sitting under the table talking to himself, able now to handle both academics and social situations. I called his parents and suggested they explore and also urge our psychologist to investigate the possibilities of a Neurologically Impaired class for him. The nystagmus in his eyes, his awkward gait, the many reversals were all indications, soft signs, of some sort of neurological involvement. One more year, particularly in the spacious new school building with its own swimming pool, would have helped, would have solidified all he had gained, but Rufus would be okay either way, I thought.

Jamie, little Jamie. I held him as often as I could and praised him when he wrote and said, "My name is Jamie Walker." He had written that first a year ago; the only other things he had written since were his address and his phone number. Jamie was never going to be "all right," but he had a large, warm, supportive family, a mother and father and four older brothers who took him with them when they went fishing or even to the movies. Whatever happened at school, Jamie would be all right at home.

Hannah. She was almost pretty now. Rufus had instigated what he called (to my great pleasure) Wait Watchers. Under his direction we all got weighed each Monday and Thursday morning. I had brought in scales, and twice a week we all took off our shoes and Rufus weighed us while Brian recorded the results on a chart on the wall. We had all lost a little weight, but Hannah lost twenty pounds.

Now, too, she had five new dresses. A woman had called me one day at school and identified herself only as Hannah's godmother. She said she was visiting the Rosnics and couldn't get over the changes in Hannah. She was excited and pleased and wanted to know if it would be all right to buy Hannah some new clothes. All right? It was marvelous. So now Hannah had a new dress for each day, and Mrs. Rosnic kept them crisp and clean. Hannah's hair had almost grown back and it was soft and silky and bright and her eyes remained blue and clear and beautiful. She had come so far, and now I poured every extra bit of energy I could find into teaching her all that I could. But even so, she remained vulnerable.

While Patty was absent, the Director sent Janie and Barbara Lasky to our room in the afternoon. Barbara was no problem; she sat in the sun contentedly, combing her hair with pieces from the erector set, and I let her sit. But Janie could not be left alone. By herself, she wound her hands around her throat and pressed her thumbs against her larynx. Her hands were amazingly strong, and after she had wrung her neck hard enough to leave deep red welts and make herself vomit, I kept her beside me.

There was never time in the morning now for math, so in the afternoon we all gathered at the two round tables and worked on math problems. Brian and Rufus were doing a unit on measurement in their workbooks; I tried to make it more meaningful by having them measure the room, the windows, their pencils and books. They did pretty well, helping each other with the rulers and yardsticks.

The rest of us added and subtracted, joined and separated sets of beads, bottle caps, and buttons. Jamie sorted marbles into the muffin tin. Sorting is the beginning of arithmetic.

The afternoon of the phone call from Jean Huntington, I went back to my class and took over from the Director, who was looking more tired

than I'd ever seen her. I explained about the call
and said I'd bring in a letter the next day.

She nodded and said she'd do what she could,
but the way she said it did little to raise my
hopes.

I sat back down with the girls, Hannah and
Janie on either side of me. I had brought in my
grandmother's button box. As a child, this same
painted-tin button box had been a source of en-
chantment. It was kept for special times, when I
was sick or when there had been a long, long
period of rain. During difficult days, when hours
passed slowly, my mother brought out the button
box. Now I laid out three round mother-of-pearl
buttons and two made of black jet. Just the physical feel of the cool stones was a pleasure.

"How many altogether?" I asked.

Without warning, Janie swept the pearl and jet
buttons off the table and cradled them in her
hands. I had no idea what she would do with
them: throw them, eat them, run away?

Instead she turned and pulled one of my hands
toward her, opening my palm. "One, two, three,
four, five."

I was amazed. Tired as I was, I could feel a
physical jolt of pleasure. "Good for you," I said.
"Good for you, lovey. That's exactly right."

Crash. The whole button box was on the floor
and Hannah was on her feet, shouting at me.
"You not call her that! She not lovey. I lovey. You
not even know her!"

"Hannah, Hannah," I said, weariness blurring my eyes. "You're right. I'm sorry. But come on, now, there's room for lots of 'loveys' in the world."

Not in Hannah's world.

That night when I wrote the letter to the Board for their meeting the following evening, I tried to combine professional knowledge with my urgent desire to teach. But fatigue took over and what came out seemed like a stilted plea.

I turned in the letter the next morning and then called Ted to check on Patty.

She was better; her fever was down and the black splitting headaches had eased. I told Ted about Janie, knowing Patty would be pleased—and then added that I had written my letter of appeal.

Ted didn't approve. "You should strike, damn it. The other teachers would support you—and rumors must be filtering out because a couple of mothers have called here, trying to sound Patty out on what to do. They'd organize. Look, Patty isn't up to it, but I can help you get started. First thing is to get a petition—"

I interrupted. "Ted, I can't do that. This place is a shambles now with Patty out and so many kids sick or just coming back. The Director is doing four jobs at once. It's already the beginning of June, almost the end of the year. I can't tear up the school even more, with the move to the new school planned for fall. Besides," I said honestly, "it's not my style. I wouldn't even know how to begin to strike."

"Yeah," Ted grunted. "That's the worst of it. You're right. It's not your style. Listen, I gotta go. Keep in touch, okay?"

I always read to the children in the afternoon. After lunch I'd get down on the rug or mats where they rested and read aloud to them. At first I read them short stories from various storybooks, but this year, as I became more and more aware of their intelligence and potential, I began to read whole books. My children ranged in age from eight to twelve, but because they were reading below grade level, the stories in their reading books were always about younger children. They needed to hear about children their own age, what these children were like, what kind of problems they encountered and dealt with.

I discussed it at staff meeting. Our psychiatrist was skeptical about the children's ability to maintain an interest over the extended period it took to read a book a chapter or two at a time. The Director and the psychologist doubted whether they would be able to remember what was happening from day to day. But psychiatrist, psychologist, and Director were wrong—and they were the first to admit it and be pleased by the rapt attention of the children as I read to them each day after lunch.

Brian, Rufus, and Hannah (Jamie just cuddled close) not only remembered the facts, they related to the children in the book and made judgments and interpretations. I was finding out what I had suspected all along. We need to teach emotionally disturbed children more rather than less. Because of their fears, their inhibitions, their bizarre traits, we tend to underestimate them. But learning is therapeutic; the ability to handle knowledge is comforting, particularly for children who have such difficulty in dealing with emotion.

We had finished *The Secret Garden*, which they had all loved. Now we were reading a book called *Peter and His Horse*. It was about a boy, ten years old, who lived close to a gentleman who raised Thoroughbred horses. Peter began to help train a colt named Star—and became more effective with him than any of the adult trainers. Peter loved Star, racing to see him as soon as his chores were done. Star responded and could sense when Peter was on his way and whinnied and trotted to the gate to wait for him.

Brian, Rufus, and Hannah were fascinated by this. Each longed for some sort of pet of his own, so they understood how Peter felt and they were delighted that Star also loved Peter.

Peter trained Star carefully each day, readying him for the County Horse Show. Everyone was excited. Surely Star would win, he was so beautiful and Peter had trained him to perform so well. Then, just the day before the show, Peter fell on his way to Star and broke his leg. He had to go to the hospital and have a cast put on his leg. Peter wouldn't be able to go to the horse show.

Hannah and Brian both moaned.

"Read. Hurry up, Mary. Find out what happens," said Rufus, unable to stand the suspense.

The man who owned Star took him to the show. Everyone agreed that that's what Peter would want. Star should have his chance to win the blue ribbon.

Star's owner groomed him carefully, but when Star entered the ring he forgot all his training.

"Oh, boy," said Hannah. "Oh, boy."

Instead of doing what he was supposed to do, Star trotted faster and faster around the ring, tossing his head from side to side, searching for Peter.

The judges dismissed him, and his owner took Star back home in disgrace.

Peter came home from the hospital a few days later, but the man who owned Star wouldn't let Peter even see the horse. He was angry with Peter; he told Peter he had made Star too dependent on him and done Star more harm than good.

When I finished the chapter we sat silently. This was unexpected. The thought that you could hurt a pet by too much or the wrong kind of loving was a new idea, one that we had never talked about.

Hannah broke the silence. "That Star, him bad. He just like kids in Patty's class. He good if Peter there. They good when Patty there. They not good when she gone. That both their trouble."

I was amazed at her reaction. I knew she was

both intelligent and aware, but I hadn't realized how far she was able to go.

Brian said, "Peter didn't mean to be bad to Star, Mary, did he? He didn't want to hurt him. I think it was like that man said. Star just got—what was that word, Mary?"

"Dependent," said Rufus, before I had a chance.

"Yeah. Star got dependent on Peter."

Brian and Hannah and Rufus solemnly nodded their heads in agreement.

"And Patty's class?" I asked. "You think they're like Star? They're too dependent on Patty?"

"Yup," said Hannah. "That just like them. They too de-pen-dent. Patty got to fix them up. Make them . . ." She stopped. She had no word for what she meant.

"Independent," I said softly.

But the children had already left the table—and it didn't matter. Knowing the word was not important; understanding the feeling was what counted.

I put the marker in the book and closed it for the day. The sun still shone outside. Everything was still in its accustomed place in our classroom, but I felt as though some miracle had occurred there.

These children—these marvelous, fascinating, wonderful children—had not only understood and followed what was happening in the book we were reading, they had taken the ideas out of the book, generalized, and applied the concepts to what was happening in their own lives. Nowhere, nowhere in the world, are there any miracles that can come close to those of children.

21

"A teacher's aide?" I said.

I stood in the Director's office after lunch the next day as she handed me back the letter I had given her for the Board.

"Yes," she said, pushing back her white hair, a pulse beating just below the strong cords in her neck. "That's the compromise the Board came up with last night. You don't have the credentials to qualify as a teacher. On the other hand, we all know how devoted you are to the school and that you're good with the children."

I barely heard her. A teacher's aide.

"What—what would I do as a teacher's aide?"

This annoyed the Director and she snapped, "Just what it says. Be an aide to a teacher. Look, Mary, I know that this may be hard for you to swallow. You've been treated as though you actually were a teacher for so long. But the facts are, you're not. You're not even a college graduate, to be absolutely frank. There is no way the state could accept you as part of the staff. I'm sorry, but that's just the way it is."

I turned toward the door, with no thought but to get out of the room, back to the children.

"Mary"—the Director's voice softened—"I'm sorry. I didn't mean to speak so strongly. We'll try to work something out. Maybe you could work in a classroom with a sliding door, adjacent to a real teacher."

"A real teacher. Ah-h. Yes, of course."

I was grateful to her for that phrase. Anger fired in my stomach and blazed its way to my head, burning away wisps of sadness and self-pity. To hell with her. And the Board. And the school.

But it wasn't easy. The school meant the children.

I walked back to my room. In the hall, from the other classrooms, and now here in my own room, the sounds of children swirled around me.

I sat down by the window and Hannah said, "You gone long time, teacher. Now read."

She brought me the book and as I took it from her I couldn't help but think, At least I'd still be here with you, lovey. If I stayed as a teacher's aide, this learning could keep going on. . . .

"Mary," said Rufus. "You're not reading. Are you okay?"

"Oh," I said, my mind coming back. "Yeah, sure. Well, actually, not tip-top, but pretty good. Now let's see, where are we?"

"Star didn't win anything at the horse show. The man is mad at Peter 'cause Star got de-pen-dent," said Brian.

"Right. Okay, now look. We're almost done. Only two more chapters."

The children settled in close to me on the rug and I read. "The days went very slowly now that Peter was no longer allowed to see Star. . . ."

It was a short chapter and a sad one. This was even harder to understand than the previous chapter. Punishments in our room never lasted longer than a day. Whatever had occurred was over by nightfall and you started the next day clean. But now, in this book, more than a week had passed. The man was still angry. Peter was still not allowed to see Star.

I said, "What do you think will happen next?"

Usually Rufus or Hannah would jump to the question, knowing exactly what they thought would happen. Right or wrong, they were willing to project, to commit themselves to how they thought it would all turn out. Brian took a little more time, but usually he too was willing to hazard a guess.

But not now. They looked at me silently, sadly.

I asked, "How could it have been different?"

It was Brian who answered first this time. Not answering the question directly, going around a bit, but still thinking and trying to communicate his thoughts.

"It wasn't Peter's fault. He didn't mean to. . . . If that horse had had more control he would of been all right."

Rufus disagreed. "But Peter shouldn't let him get so dependent. He should of made him have control. 'Member, Mary? You used to say, 'If you can't control yourself, I'll help you.' First you had

to do it, but then you made us do it. 'Member
that? Boy, you grabbed Jamie hard when he kept
running away and you said to him, 'If you can't
control yourself, I'll help you,' and then when he
kicked you took off his shoes and just held on till
he could control himself."

I looked at Jamie for affirmation, but Jamie
never paid attention to words. He just sat quietly,
leaning against my arm, turning one of the buttons in his hand.

Brian said, "If that Star got control, then he
wouldn't've kept looking for Peter. He wouldn't
need him any more."

Hannah burst out, "No. That not right. Star *always* need Peter. He love him. He just not need
him *all* time."

Maybe that's it, I thought. We all need each
other, but if we have some inner controls, we
don't need each other quite so desperately. Not
all time.

22

"How long will it take?" I said to the curriculum adviser out at college.

He looked at me quizzically. "You mean right now?"

"No, altogether. Sorry, I don't mean to rush you."

"You've asked that before."

"I know. But now I need it in black and white. How long if I take night courses? And how long if I become a regular day student?"

"But I thought you said you couldn't—"

"Please. Look, let's just write it down."

"All right." Efficiency took over and the dry little man who was in charge of curriculum credits got out ruled paper and pencil and lined them up precisely in front of him. He placed my transcript to his left and the college catalog to his right. "Now. You have sixty-eight credits at the present time. You'll have six more, if you pass your exam, heh-heh. Uh, sorry. So that will be seventy-four. You need one hundred and twenty-four to graduate, all in the proper departments and correct courses, naturally. Not much leeway there. Hmm. But—never mind. Let's not worry about that now. Let's say you take another three evening courses in the fall—that's six more credits—and another three courses in the spring term for six additional credits. That'll give you twelve more credits or eighty-six altogether."

I felt as if I were going out of my head. I wanted to shout at the poor little man, Hurry up, just tell me what I asked, the difference between the two ways. How could I be so unhurried with the children and so impatient now? I knew how: because this had absolutely nothing to do with education or learning, the children's or my own. That's how!

"Now let's figure that out here. Seventy-four from one hundred and twenty-four leaves fifty." He smiled at me. "Comes out even. A nice round figure. Fifty. That's, let's see, a little over four years. Of course, there's summer school. . . ."

I controlled my voice, knowing I couldn't hurry him. "Let's forget summer school for now. We can do that later. Now suppose I came full time in the fall."

"Well, you'd still have the same seventy-four credits, so we'll begin there. This, of course, is assuming you pass the entrance exams. Heh-heh. Now the regular semester load is fifteen credits. That odd credit is one for gym. Heh-heh-heh-heh."

I thought I might bop his shiny little head. Take all his semester credits and . . . No, no. Listen, now. He's finished with gym.

"So—fifteen credits a term, that would be thirty a year. Now how many did we say you needed?"

"Fifty."

"Ah, yes. Have it right here. Fifty, a nice round number. So thirty from fifty leaves twenty. About a year and a half, if you push a little. Of course, when we figure in summer school. . . ."

"Thank you. Thank you very much. I'll let you know."

Four years of classes at night, but I could stay on at our school, keep on with the children, keep Hannah going, earn my small but adequate salary.

Or a year and a half, maybe less, going full time, to get my teaching credentials, the magical union papers that would automatically make me a "real teacher." But there would be no children, no Hannah—and no salary, although I did have enough saved to manage on.

I still didn't know what I was going to do, but at least the alternatives were getting clearer.

23

It was so hot that beads of perspiration were forming on the children's foreheads by nine thirty in the morning.

Circle was quiet. No games, just a few songs. The latest substitute for Patty's class had lasted three days now and Patty herself was due back tomorrow, so the worst was over.

Still, it would be a long, hot day. The air was heavy, and as we finished Best and Worst, Rufus wiped first his forehead and then his glasses. "Can't we just finish the book now, Mary? I don't feel like doing my reading. It's too hot and we've only got a little left."

I considered and concluded that Rufus was right. We might as well stay at the table and finish the last chapter. I opened the doors to stir whatever air currents there were and began to read.

It was a happy chapter, and gradually the children forgot the heat and their discomfort as the world of Peter and Star again became real.

Star's owner finally relented and let Peter see

Star again. Both the boy and the horse were over-joyed and Peter resolved not to make the mistake he had made before. Instead of jealously keeping Star to himself, he urged the other men in the stable to work with Star and also helped with some of the other horses. Star gradually became used to other people and this time was ready for the state horse show.

The day before the show, Peter groomed Star until his coat glistened and his mane was tawny and smooth. But Peter's leg wasn't quite healed and one of the other trainers took Star into the ring. Peter watched from the sidelines, holding his breath, but Star performed perfectly, trotting around the ring, holding his head high and still. On the final page Star won the blue ribbon—and the owner gave it to Peter, telling him he deserved it as much as Star.

Hannah, Brian, and Rufus all sighed in hap-piness.

"Is good book, teacher."

"Read that last page, that part where Star wins the blue ribbon, again, Mary."

I knew how they felt—it was good, too good to end. Besides, when I stopped reading, my own problems and pending decisions came crowding in. I read the last page again.

This time when we finished Rufus said, "Star's okay now. At that last show he could control his head. He didn't need to keep looking for Peter. I don't think he even thought about controlling it.

It's just on his inside now and he doesn't need to think."

"And Peter, he's all right," said Brian. "He's not hurting Star any more."

"Him not mean hurt Star. Him let Star go now. Like mices," sighed Hannah.

Like children. Like any kind of loving.

"It's not easy," I said, "to learn all that."

Jamie nuzzled his head against my arm and then, sensing that no one was quite ready to start work yet, he climbed into my lap.

"It takes a long time to learn. A really long time. I was scared like that, like Star, for a long time." Rufus turned to me. "Do you remember how scared I was when I first came?"

"I remember, Ruf. I remember just the way you were. You wore a dark blue suit—"

"And I had that giant brown briefcase. Remember that briefcase? And look, this is how I walked. . . ."

Rufus got up and walked to the door, looking like the Rufus we knew, but when he turned around this Rufus was gone and in his place was a stiff, frightened, almost mechanical boy. He moved his legs rigidly as he walked toward us.

"I walked in the room like this and then I put my briefcase in front so nobody would see me. Anyway, I pretended nobody could see me. I was so scared. I tried to throw up. I thought you'd send me home if I threw up. Do you remember the pain in my stomach?"

"I do, Rufus." There was so much I remembered. It seemed such a short time ago. Why did I have this big lump in my throat?

Brian said, "And me. I've been here longest. Nobody else was here then. Only you, Mary. This is how I came in. ..."

Brian edged his way to the door and then turned swiftly, running, flapping, squawking out a struggled "awk-awk."

"That's the way I came. And listen to this: 'Horyutdy. Mgldeseyu.' That's how I used to talk."

Hannah said, "Why you talk funny like that, Bri-an? That dumb."

Brian paused and looked at Hannah. "I don't know," he said. "I don't know why. I was different then."

Hannah considered. "That okay. I dumb once too. Carl, Grandpa say I retard."

The boys looked at her. I looked at her. I wished there were some sort of recorder or another person in the room. It was hard for me to believe that this was actually happening—that these children knew, had known all along, what they had been like, who they were—and, more than that, recognized who they had become.

Hannah had to do it. I knew she had to do it. I wished she wouldn't, but if the boys had acted out their beginnings, Hannah would too.

She crouched on her hands and knees and began rocking back and forth, back and forth, building the momentum to a crescendo—and then she brought her head down toward the floor.

"Hannah!" I cried, not able to stand any more. "Don't. Don't do that!"

But her head had barely touched the floor. She had stopped the downward thrust just in time so that her forehead barely grazed the tiles. Now she was up, heading for the closet. She went inside, pulling the doors closed behind her.

The boys and I sat staring at the tightly shut doors. Then a crack appeared, then a larger one, then Hannah's head came round the door. "See, Bri-an. I not dumb now. Not retard." She opened the door, stepped all the way out, and said with absolute assurance, "I lovey now."

The emotion in the room was so high I wondered how we could stay there the rest of the day. Whatever we did would be anticlimactic. I gave Jamie a little extra hug, then got up and began to rearrange the tables and chairs. Maybe we could go outside, find Henry—

But Hannah wasn't done. She tugged my arm, tugged hard, and said, loud enough so the boys could hear, "What you like, teacher? Nobody know you when you come here."

Did she mean what had I been like in the beginning? Did she think that I could do what they had done and act out my beginnings? Well, I couldn't. I couldn't talk about how I felt, how I had been....

"It was a long, long time ago," I said.

Hannah nodded.

"I mean a really long time ago. Six years." I looked at her. "You were only two."

Hannah nodded again. Somehow I found myself moving to the door.

"I didn't know anything about teaching—and not very much about myself." I reached the door and turned around.

Almost against my will I could feel my steps becoming hesitant, my shoulders curving slightly downward, my voice lower, less sure.

"I only knew I wanted to learn, to begin to understand, to teach here. . . ."

Suddenly I realized that the children were staring at me. "Well," I said, straightening. "That was quite a while ago."

But Hannah understood it and she put it into the words I couldn't find. "You shrimpy," she said. "You shrimpy teacher when you come here."

She pointed to the picture that hung on the front wall by our blackboard. It was the painting she had given me for a Valentine present. There the sun shone and the teacher sailed across the grass in her sneakers, with her skirt spread wide as though the world could be crossed in a minute, and all the time the big red blob that was her heart rested comfortably on the outside of her shirt.

"That teacher," she said, "not shrimpy any more."

It was clear now. Hannah had made it clear to me. I couldn't be a teacher's aide again. I couldn't go back. There was no way I could deliberately choose to be shrimpy again.

24

The sounds of children ran through my head day and night, blurring thoughts, drowning sleep. Their words, their stories, their songs, their shouts, whoops, yells, cries of happiness and pain mixed with my own heartbeats. When I spoke my voice seemed strange to me, muted, distant, layered between the noises of the children.

"Are you sure?" Ted asked on the night before the last day. We were having a picnic at school the next day, and I was at Patty's house, packing supplies in her Volkswagen bus. Ted spoke quickly while Patty was in the house getting another carton. "Somehow," he continued, "it doesn't seem right that you won't have a chance to teach at the new school, have a few decent facilities for a change. . . . Listen, Patty won't ask you, she says it's an insult, but she'd love to have you teach with her, you know that. And the teacher's aide thing—that would be in name only."

"I know," I said. "Thank you. Patty, too. There's nobody I'd rather work with, but I've been thinking that someday I may want to work in a public school, and if I do I'll have to have certification. Now seems like the best time to do it."

Was that really my voice, so cool and calm? My reasoned argument?

Who was I kidding? What was I doing? How could I last two days, much less two years?

But the hardest part was over—or anyway, that's what I told myself. I'd made the decision, filled out the application blanks for college, even paid the first installment on tuition. I'd written the Board, spoken to the Director; everything was set. Almost everything. I would tell the children as casually as I could just before they left for the summer.

The morning of June nineteenth dawned bright and beautiful. It was the last school day of the year, but more important than that, it was Hannah's birthday. She was nine years old today. Nine years old and this was going to be her first party. There had never been anyone to invite before.

As I ate breakfast I listened carefully to the weather report: 80 percent chance of rain and thunderstorms by afternoon. But now, at eight in the morning, there wasn't a cloud in the sky. It seemed like a good omen; the sun should shine on Hannah's birthday.

She might never have had a party before, but this one was going to make up for it, in size anyway. The whole school was coming. A picnic on the last day was a tradition at the school, and now fate conspired to have Hannah's birthday fall on that same day. All I had to do was help it along a little.

We had three cakes baked, all saying HAPPY BIRTHDAY, HANNAH in pink letters. We had candles, balloons, paper tablecloths, party hats, and presents. Patty and I had bought out Woolworth's, and now we had a stack of brightly wrapped presents two feet high: bubble bath, crayons, pencils, paper, a coloring book, a jump rope, a pair of socks, a new shirt. I had been tempted by the goldfish and the gerbils but, remembering Cougar, I'd passed them up in favor of a small gold heart on a thin gold chain set with a red stone to match Hannah's ring from the dentist.

The rest of the presents could wait till lunch, but I handed her the little package with the necklace as soon as she came to school.

"Happy, happy birthday, Hannah," I said, hugging her and then fastening the chain around her neck.

"Is beautiful, teacher. Just like dentist doctor ring."

"Just like your heart," I said. "Only yours is bigger."

But Hannah couldn't bear to get a present and not give one. She searched the room for something to give me—until she spotted the little bottle of teeth that still sat on my table. Happily she trotted to get them and brought them back to me.

"Here. My tooths from dentist doctor. You

keep." Her smile lighted the whole corner of the room. "Forever," she said.

Everyone gathered in the parking lot at eleven o'clock. There were thirty or forty of us: children, teachers, volunteers, the Director, even some of the mothers and younger brothers and sisters. Henry was there with a bunch of his prettiest roses. Mrs. Rosnic was meeting us at the park with Helen and the ice cream.

"Boy," I whispered to Hannah. "What a party you're going to have!"

Hannah was radiant, her cheeks flushed with excitement, her eyes bluer than ever, matching her new dress. The boys were almost as excited as Hannah.

"Did you bring the cake, Mary? Did you?"

"Shh, it's a surprise. Of course."

"And the candles? Did you get nine candles?"

"Yes. Even more. Stop worrying, Bri. We've got everything."

And it truly seemed as if we did. When we got to the little state park, the children tumbled out of the cars and ran across the grassy fields down to the lake. Wild ducks had made the lake their own reservation and now they squawked in surprise at the arrival of the children. But we had brought bags of bread crusts and the birds quieted as the children fed them.

Mothers and teachers took turns watching the children and unpacking the food. Brian, Rufus, and I sat on one of the picnic tables blowing up balloons, handing them out to whoever wanted one.

I loved to see the children running free, some down by the lake, some across the fields, some just carrying food from the car. The green fields were splashed with the colors of the children's clothes and the bright blue sky was dotted with balloons. I blinked my eyes to focus, to snap the shutter of my mind; it was a picture I would like to keep forever.

At lunch we ate our sandwiches. Hannah ate, too—daintily, almost elegantly. We toasted Hannah with our lemonade and then carried in the birthday cakes—all three, each with ten candles. Nine for each year and one to grow on.

Ah, Hannah. One to grow on.

Hannah blew out the candles, one cake at a time, and Mrs. Rosnic stood beside her dishing ice cream into paper bowls. It was hard to tell which one looked happier. I suddenly realized that in all the times I had seen Mrs. Rosnic, I had never seen her smile before. Now, wreathed in happiness, their faces were amazingly alike, and I went and stood beside them.

Hannah's hair was soft and clean and shone like a polished penny. The skin on her arms, neck, and face was smooth and creamy and just now her cheeks were pink with excitement. Her eyes were the same startling combination of blues—a light cornflower blue on the surface, then darker layers underneath, down to a vivid deep blue. Hannah had always had an easy, airy grace, but now her new slenderness and new clothes added a delicacy and charm. Hannah seemed prettier to me than any Blue Fairy could ever be.

Mrs. Rosnic touched my arm, still smiling, and gestured toward Hannah, whispering, "Who could have thought! Is so pretty!"

I smiled too—who could help it?—and whispered back, "Yes, she is, and so are you."

After lunch we rode back to the school packed between balloons, remnants of potato chips, paper, and ribbon. Hannah had folded each piece of paper and ribbon, refusing to give up even the tiniest scrap.

Mrs. Rosnic left for home directly from the picnic. I had said to Hannah, "You can leave now too, lovey. You don't need to come all the way back to school."

But Hannah shook her head and climbed into her usual spot in the front seat, with Rufus, Brian, and Jamie in the back. She had parted with her presents and the remains of the cake; Mrs. Rosnic had these carefully stored in her car. Hannah evidently wanted one last ride with the boys before the year ended—and so did I. This was the last time I would ride surrounded by the children, and I drove as slowly as I could, savoring each second.

We were late. The buses and cars and even Brian's taxi were already lining up in the driveway when we got back to school.

There was a distant rumble of thunder as we ran down to our room. The Director was calling,

"Hurry up, now, children. It's time to go. Your buses are waiting."

I piled the children's arms with the paintings and papers they had done during the year. Hannah had so many, she had to make two trips. Then they gathered on the little stoop outside our classroom and I kissed each one, each special one.

"Listen, now," I said. "You have a good summer and a good year. I'm probably going to be going to school myself in the fall, so I won't be seeing you for a while. But I'll be thinking about you and I know you'll be doing just fine."

The thunder was louder; the drivers were honking; fall was a long way off. The news that I wouldn't be back scarcely seemed important.

"Go on now," I said. "Hurry, before the rain comes."

The children ran for their buses, arms overflowing with papers, still calling good-byes.

The bus drivers were jockeying for position in line, eager to have the children board, anxious to leave before the storm broke.

Rufus was in the first bus, waving happily with Jamie beside him. Brian was in a taxi just a little farther on, his sweet, intelligent face pressed tight against the window.

I took a step out from the door. "Good luck, Bri. Good luck in school."

He nodded, pressing his face tighter against the rolled-up window, almost managing a smile. And then he too was gone.

Hannah? Where was she? There were only two

buses left and they were starting to move now, the other children still calling their good-byes through half-open windows. I stood on the stoop, searching for Hannah, for one last glimpse of her. And then suddenly I saw her.

She was kneeling on a seat by the window. As she passed our door, she called out. Her voice mingled with the other children's as they shouted their farewells: "Good-bye, Patty. Good-bye, Mary. Good-bye, Ellen. 'Bye, teacher. . . ."

But I heard, or thought I did, one high sweet call above the rest, "Good-bye, now. Good-bye now, lovey."

Epilogue

I have never gone back to the school—it would have been too painful for me and unfair to the children—but I've kept track of them, and now they are almost grown.

Brian has finished high school and has a job on a small newspaper. His memory for batting averages, names, and records is put to good use in the sports department.

Rufus is almost six feet tall. He is in his third year in high school and is getting good grades. During the summer he works as a junior counselor at a camp for handicapped children.

Jamie is living at home and going to a prevocational training program preparing for a sheltered workshop.

Hannah has moved south. Grandpa died and Mrs. Rosnic sold the house and headed for Florida with the three children to join her longtime friend, Hannah's godmother. Hannah entered a day school with a good reputation for helping children with emotional problems. At first she was put in a class headed by a male teacher, but Hannah grew silent and withdrawn. She was transferred, and under the tutelage of a young, capable woman, Hannah once again began to grow. At last report, her progress was good. She has developed a talent for working with the younger children and often assists in the primary grades, particularly the dance classes.

I finished college with a bachelor's degree in education and then a master's in learning disabilities. I continue to work with children, primarily those with emotional or learning problems, in both public school and private practice.

About the Author

Mary MacCracken is a certified special education teacher who holds a masters degree in learning disabilities. She has taught emotionally disturbed children in both public and private schools. In addition, the author is the mother of three children. Ms. MacCracken has also written the celebrated NAL publication A CIRCLE OF CHILDREN.

More SIGNET Books of Special Interest

NAL/ABRAMS BOOKS
ON ART, CRAFT AND SPORTS

*in beautiful, large format, special
concise editions—lavishly illustrated
with many full-color plates.*
